WHAT WORKS ABOUT DOING GOOD?

"Pay it forward" is a familiar concept. People talk about the idea and smile. Bryan Douglas was different. He thought the idea sounded so good that he wanted to test it out. So he actually did it. And the experience changed his life and positively impacted the lives of others.

The interesting thing is, Bryan didn't look for people who were really down and out. He just looked for people who needed a hand. How did he do that? He put a notice on Craigslist! Then, when he got some responses, he went out and did what he said he would—he helped people and asked only that someday they might do something for someone else.

His experience was strong enough that it moved him to write a book based on a direct experience of doing good. More than just his story, it provides the supporting evidence of the good inherent in doing good based on observable results. He financed it out of his own pocket, which could be considered another demonstration of paying it forward with little expectation other than it might inspire someone else to do what he did—in their own way, of course.

Doing Good Works! is a simple and clear description and discussion of the benefit for the world, the recipient, and the one providing the "good" work. Extraordinary quotes from ordinary people punctuate each chapter. Ideas for little things you can do in a moment that produce positive movement abound. Inspiration for doing good is on every page—not because anyone is trying to   simply because it is clear that doing good...works!

ABOUT THE AUTHORS

Bryan Douglas is twenty-nine years old, and lives in Pittsburgh (although you never know where he might turn up to lend a helping hand!).

Sean Elliot Martin is a man of many interests, not the least of which is volunteer service. He applies his PhD in English by teaching literature and composition at Duquesne University, Point Park University, and The Art Institute of Pittsburgh. He also teaches, and is Grandmaster of a new martial art, Kage-Essensu survival combat, which qualifies him to teach self-defense at charitable organizations, something he does as a volunteer. Sean writes lyrics and melody for musical projects, and has had his wood sculpture featured at the Pittsburgh Renaissance Festival. He lives in the borough of Dormont, PA, and is working to make time to be more involved with the local community. He is one of Bryan's close friends.

DOING GOOD WORKS!

Michele,

Small acts really do make the Biggest difference!

Bryan

DOING GOOD WORKS!

Small Acts That Make a Big Difference

BRYAN DOUGLAS

WITH Sean Elliot Martin

Think Big Press

Bethel Park, PA

Doing Good Works
Small Acts that Make a Big Difference

First Edition

7288 Baptist Road, #136
Bethel Park, PA 15102
contact@doinggoodworks.org

Printed in the United States of America

Publisher's Cataloging-in-Publication Data

Douglas, Bryan.
    Doing good works! : small acts that make a big difference / Bryan
    Douglas with Sean Elliot Martin. -- Bethel Park, PA : Think Big
    Press, c2009.

        p. ; cm.
        ISBN: 978-0-9841890-7-6

        1. Altruism. 2. Helping behavior. 3. Kindness. 4. Conduct of
    life. I. Martin, Sean Elliot. II. Title.

BJ1474 .D68 2009   2009934025
171/.8--dc22   0910

Book Cover & Interior Design: Ghislain Viau
Book Consultant: Ellen Reid
Editor: Pamela Guerreri

DEDICATION

It is difficult to know where to begin in terms of dedicating this book and thanking those who helped in so many ways. Perhaps the best thing to do is to thank literally everyone in the world. This book would not exist exactly as it is, for better or worse, if all of the people in the world were not exactly who and what they are. A variety of family, friends, strangers, scholars, and leaders has taught us directly and indirectly over the years. We are eternally grateful to each one of them.

CONTENTS

Beginning today ... treat everyone you meet as if he or she were going to be dead by midnight. Extend to them all the care, kindness, and understanding you can muster, and do so with no thought of any reward. Your life will never be the same again.
—Og Mandino

Chapter One

STARTING OUT

D o you think it's possible to change the world? Do you think you have the ability to change the world? How about someone you know? Do you think anyone you know has what it takes? The great educator Horace Mann once urged everyone to "Be ashamed to die until you have won some victory for humanity." Some people find this idea to be inspirational. Most people I have talked to about this quote see it as quite intimidating, even overwhelming. That is probably because they are assuming that the victory must be a massive victory, something that will be recorded in history books.

However, Mann doesn't indicate the scope of the victory. He merely says "some victory." What kind of victory can you win for humanity? Can you invent something to help people with physical limitations? Can you lead peace efforts between two warring countries? Any major accomplishment in history was once nothing more than a dream in the mind of a human being just like you. However, if neither inventing nor diplomacy is your speed, how about raising your kids to be decent, compassionate citizens? How about creating something that can inspire a few people to live better lives? Serving a meal to the homeless or taking care of abandoned animals is a wonderful victory for the forces of good. So is simply being the best person you can be.

I certainly claim no greater wisdom or insight than anyone else, but I know that I have an overwhelming drive to apply my *Practical Imagination* to help others in any way that I can. There are actually two of us working on this book. One prefers to remain anonymous (using a pen name), so I am making minor adjustments to the writing to see to his wishes. Mainly, I am mixing in our voices to blur the line between us, making the details of our lives and backgrounds a bit fuzzy. As a result, you will see intentional shifts between "I" and "we" in the narrative, and true personal notes that may be from either of us.

Without giving too much away, I will mention that one of us is a successful businessman. One of us has a PhD and the other has a high school education. Both of us have traveled extensively, meeting people from a variety of backgrounds and cultures. Both of us have been involved with charities. One of us has a criminal record from long ago. One of us had a drinking problem. One of us is a martial arts instructor with twenty-eight years in the martial arts. One of us has been injured in alcohol-related crashes. One of us has read numerous books on success. One of us has battled with drugs. One of us ran away at seventeen years old. One of us has struggled with depression and mild OCD. One of us has been labeled "bipolar." Both of us have had a huge variety of good and bad experiences. Both of us have seen acts of horrible violence and injury, as well as incredible acts of bravery and kindness. Both of us have experienced some sort of poverty. Both of us have spent hundreds of hours doing volunteer work and getting to know people.

It is not important who has experienced what. We are close friends who have vastly different experiences and personalities. The main thing we have in common is our passion for making a difference and helping others to do the same. Between the two of us, we have some experience to bring to this project. Most importantly, we learned from these experiences, making major improvements in our lives and in the lives of those around us. We desperately want to help others to do the same, and this book is the best strategy we can come up with at the moment. We are still learning and improving ourselves. To a great extent, we are thinking of our own shortcomings and bad habits as we write the words of this project. We may need this book more than many of our readers need it, and we will try very hard to follow our own suggestions.

I recently made a trip to Chicago for a weekend of good deeds. The idea was spontaneous and simple: go to another city and spend one weekend helping people there. Some of the results were quite unexpected. I randomly chose Chicago and decided which weekend I would go. Then, I went on the Internet to ask who in Chicago needed help that weekend. It didn't take long to get it narrowed down to five sincere requests for help, and off I went! It was one of the greatest experiences of my life. I documented the whole thing via digital camcorder and still photos, and then put it on the Internet to try to encourage others to do similar things—whatever was in their hearts and worked for them. I wanted to try to plant the seed of good and see what would happen, hoping that the "random acts of kindness" would inspire viewers. The results were more than I could have imagined. E-mails started to flood in, and six continents had hits on the video. A few people asked if it was a hoax—who in the world would stage a hoax like that?—but the general response was overwhelmingly positive.

It is not our job to know exactly how far our positive impact can go. Our job, I think, is to figure out ways that we can contribute to the world and to our own joy at the same time. Can you win a victory over the forces of negativity, anger, and depression in your own life? For whatever it is worth, I believe that you can—and you should, too. That is how all positive change starts. We don't have to change much, and we don't have to really give up anything. We don't have to totally reinvent our lives. If each of the six billion people on the planet were to create one additional "random act of kindness" per day, the ripple across the world would be powerful indeed. These are not new concepts, but they are often forgotten. What if you were to somehow help a homeless person to begin a new and productive life, requesting only that he or she "pay it forward" in return? If that woman or man were to do a similar deed and make the same request, the eventual effect would be amazing. You already know the concept, but let's try to rediscover it.

The single most common and most devastating mistake that most people around the world make on a regular basis is that they underestimate their own abilities for positive change. That's the big one. Period. I will insist upon this until the day I die (and probably after that). Most people seem to feel trapped, stuck, and at the mercy of higher or lower forces. We often play the role of the victim and / or the gambler. Either life is out to get us or the intent of fickle fate changes every day. Or maybe we believe that it is the will of other people that completely controls our lives. In any case, we usually fail to see the millions of opportunities around us that we can use to change ourselves, our lives, and our world.

Have you heard the idea that every problem creates an opportunity? It's true. Lines like "that's just the way it is" or "some things will never change" poison the minds of those who need and want change. It is "just the way it is" because everyone allows it to remain that way. "Some things never change" because we don't make them change. Let's use a rather simple but effective analogy here. When your car gets a flat, do you get it fixed, or just drive around on the rim, grumbling, "That's just the way it is"? You get it fixed, of course! The ones who bypass the grumbling or self-pitying stage and just get it fixed are the types who know how to make a difference. Some people can even look at the flat tire as an opportunity to make a new business contact at the auto shop! Perhaps part of the problem is that most people have the idea that there is a clear line between the things they can change and the things they can't. You have the power to move that line to make the "things I can change" category a whole lot bigger. That is what we want to help you to do.

It has become very popular, even fashionable, to talk about "thinking outside of the box." We will do you one better. In most cases, there *is* no "box"! The "box" itself is usually an illusion. Have you ever seen the box? What does it look like? I've never seen it. The box is a myth. Don't empower the myth by trying to think outside of something that does not exist. Focus on what you want to change in the world (which includes changes in you) and look at every single option for doing so, imposing no limitations on yourself in the brainstorming process. Then choose the options that work best for you. Don't be afraid to think big or try new things. You can only live as large as you can dream.

This book is designed to help with what we call *Practical Imagination.* Most people have come to look at imagination as the stuff of science fiction and fairy tales. That may be part of the problem of this worldwide sense of helplessness. Imagination does not just mean sitting around and drawing rainbow critters with butterfly wings, zebra bodies, and the heads of kittens (although that would be amusing, now that I think about it). Practical Imagination means acknowledging when the box does not exist, and exploring every avenue to achieve your goal of changing some aspect of the world, no matter how small, in ways that may not be entirely obvious.

If you don't believe in the power and importance of the imagination in changing the world, consult the works of Albert Einstein, who said:

> *"Imagination is everything. It is the preview of life's coming attractions."*

and

> *"Imagination is more important than knowledge. For knowledge is limited to all we now know and understand, while imagination embraces the entire world, and all there ever will be to know and understand."*

Along those lines, I understand that the great Nicola Tesla developed the idea of alternating electrical current as a result of a vision inspired by a poem.

The very nature of innovation and progress indicates that something once existed only as a vision in the mind of the creator. We are unique creatures in that we can project into the "what if," the realm of theories, possibilities, and alternative realities. If you look around the room (assuming you are indoors at the moment), please realize that pretty much everything that you see—furniture, electronics, carpet, books, walls—was once nothing more than an idea. Thoughts become things:

> *"Whatever the mind of man can conceive and believe, it can achieve. Thoughts are things!"* —Napoleon Hill

All real progress of any kind results from bringing useful actions, methods, objects, devices, and procedures out of the imagination and into the shared world. That means you can be a part of positive change in ways no one has even explored. As I am writing this book right now, I realize that, less than a month ago, this book was just a spontaneous idea.

Please take a bit of time to examine and list all of the resources available to you. Do you have a home? I don't mean necessarily owning your own house. Are you homeless, or do you have an apartment, house, or condo? If you have a place to stay, that is a valuable resource. You could possibly foster a child or an animal, take in an exchange student, or participate in an international "couch surfing" program. You could host a family member's graduation or birthday party. You could allow a charity to store a few things in a closet that you don't need. You could allow small fundraising or planning parties to happen at your place, with the understanding that the group takes care of supplies and cleanup. You would provide the space, and they'd provide everything else, and you could all be happy. That was not so bad, was it?

Do you have full use of your limbs? That is not a rhetorical question. I don't know if you do or not. I have several friends who are partially paralyzed or otherwise limited in their movement. Do you think someone like that thinks that the full use of all four limbs is anything to take for granted? If you

> " *I'm the type of person who can't live in a box. I want to do great things.* —Mike Poremski "

are able-bodied, you are blessed, and your health is a gift that deserves to be shared. You can put those hands to work packing unused medical surplus to send to less fortunate populations through charities like the Brother's Brother Foundation, or walking dogs for the Humane Society, or just helping someone carry a TV up the steps.

How you help is up to you, but please do not horde your health and vitality to yourself if you are blessed enough to have it. If you have your health and a bit of time, you can help a friend move into a new home. This is one of the most dreaded requests that people get. You know it's not going to be fun, but it's time to soldier up and get things done for your buddies. Moving is usually an ordeal, but friends can make it less physically and mentally stressful. Does helping one person to move into a new home change the world? Well, you certainly improved that person's life, and he or she is a part of the world. Your help may even prevent a serious injury. You can also save a life by being a designated driver. It may take as little as ten minutes of your time to keep a friend from being arrested, dying, or killing someone else. Changing the world often starts at home.

Your list of resources will probably be extensive when you really start to think about all that you have available: maybe a

— Idea —

Think about the greatest goal you would want to accomplish if you had unlimited resources. Then think about how you can make it happen.

home, a vehicle, a fairly healthy body, knowledge of basic tasks, life experience, insight, job skills, friends, family, contacts, the ability to read and write. No matter how you view your present state, you can probably list at least ten of your opportunities or assets that other people in the world would love to have. This means that, no matter who you are or what you have, you are a powerhouse for positive change. You have many options and resources for changing the world, changing yourself, and changing the lives of those around you for the better. The hardest part is merely deciding what to do first. Once you start thinking in this way, and then taking action, you will probably want to continue, for a number of reasons.

If you can read this, you can improve the world. For instance, you could begin by volunteering to read for people with vision problems.

The world can be a magnificent place. We all know it has problems. Problems will always exist, and complaining about them does not help. Perhaps the question is really this: Can you live with yourself knowing you did not do what you could? You decide how, when, where, and how much you want

> " *Even on my worst day, there are people who have it much worse than me, and if given the chance, I am certain they would love to trade places with me … I think about the poor people that would love to have my problems.* —Ed Buettner "

10

to participate. Our main purpose here is to explore *Practical Optimism* and *Practical Imagination* for you to apply to your own journey. We have encountered so many individuals who want to change the world and themselves. They are inspired, or at least willing to give it a shot—yet they don't know where to begin. They are in no position to donate large sums of money or weeks and months of time, but that does not mean that they are incapable of phenomenal contributions to the world. This book was created to give good people some good ideas, to show you some ways to take the time and resources you have now to change the world in ways that will make you feel wonderful without negatively affecting your own life. We are not talking about sacrifice here. Our suggestions come entirely out of real "win-win" thinking.

At this point, I am glad to say that the story of my Chicago trip has spread, and it looks like more good has come of the whole thing than I would have thought. The strangest part to me is how small the act really was. It cost a little bit of money and one weekend of my time—not a fortune, and not a major portion of my life. That is what really struck me more than anything else. It seemed like a big project when I first started out. It took a bit of work to coordinate, and the drive was exhausting (and a little scary). But it was really not that big a

---

— Idea —

Think about a problem you have, and think about why someone else might love to be in your situation.

---

deal. When I saw all of the great responses that the trip brought, I started thinking: "Man! That was actually pretty easy, and look at how much good it did!" The people I helped directly on the trip were well worth my effort, in and of themselves, but I never would have guessed that the story would inspire so many more to see that any "normal" person can make a big difference without having to sacrifice more than he or she can handle. It's not like I had to join the Peace Corps or something—now those guys deserve a pat on the back!

When I got home, I just went to work the next day and started my normal week like always. I could have sat around that weekend watching TV, eating take-out, and drinking beer, and I would have spent just as much time and money—without helping anyone. Maybe sometimes that's exactly the kind of weekend you need and want, but surely not every weekend! Guess which kind of weekend was more fulfilling?

> *Everyone has a problem. If you are not born with one, then you develop one along the road of experience in life. And we all need one another to help get us through … Seeing beyond yourself to the greater good is a challenge and a hope. It's a basic principle that we have forgotten to value, and I hope that as we become 'greener,' we also become 'warmer' to one another.* —*Larissa Kisner*

Am I a role model or some kind of guru? Absolutely not, but I think that's part of the point. If an average guy can get a "crazy" but well-intentioned thought in his head, and then make it a reality that inspires others to do likewise, maybe there is hope for all of us to make a change. I am not writing this book because I am special, but precisely because I am not!

Anyone can do the kinds of things I have done. In this spirit, we have included quotes throughout this book, and in the "More Words of Wisdom" section at the back. The vast majority of those quotes—all but four, in fact—are from "real" people with whom we have communicated directly. They come from varied backgrounds in terms of profession, education, economic status, ethnicity, age, and religion. We have included their words to emphasize the idea that everyone is equal and has something to contribute, learn, and teach.

Even if this project merely inspires you to go out and find a different book on changing the world, then that is good enough for me. We have included a list of "Suggested Readings" in the back to get you started. I am hoping you will realize, "If this dude can do it, I can do him one better!" Kick my butt at helping others! It is a contest that I could not be happier to lose.

— Idea —

Think about how a problem you face can be turned into an opportunity to help yourself and others.

If you have wisdom that you would like to share, or insights that are more accessible and useful than what I have offered here, please show me how it is done. I would love for someone to "one up" me when it comes to making a difference. I am not being sarcastic. Please jump into the game. I believe that every single person who looks at this can do at least one thing far better than I ever have. All I ask is that you show yourself and the world what you are really made of.

> *All is a gift. When one can see the gift of each person, then our view of the world is completely transformed.*
> —*Kimberly A. Clouse*

— Idea —

Pick a random person you know and write down some of that person's gifts. Share the list with that person.

Chapter Two

FOCUS ON COMMONALITY

Y ou and your world are one. This is one of the most fundamental truths, but also one of the most overlooked. Most people seem to think of the world as something that happens "out there." Sorry to break it to you, but you are the world, and the world is you. You affect the world every day, and it affects you every day. We can't avoid this, so let's quit trying. Even if you decided to stay in your home to avoid the world, your absence would affect the world in many ways. People would come looking for you to find out what was going on.

You are (at least partially) a product of your world, and it is (at least partially) a product of you. The "nature vs. nurture" debate does not even begin to interfere with this observation, because both nature and nurture are part of the world at large. Therefore, whether you think you are more a product of your genetics or your upbringing, those are both parts of this thing we call "the world." Your genetic line is part of the world. Your parents, your friends, your schools, and your experiences are all parts of the world. The world contributed to making you who and what you are. Conversely, the world has a bit of you in it: the job you do, the school you attend, and the people and animals you interact with are all affected by you.

You may even correspond with people overseas, bringing your ideas to others around the globe. One kind word via the Internet to a business associate in Europe may lead that person to be a bit more optimistic when talking to a relative who has an idea for a new project in Asia. That project may positively affect millions in Asia, and in Africa as well. It's okay that you may never know if it was you who nudged this vital change forward. You know you have put out as much positive feedback as possible. When you act in this way all the time, it becomes its own reward. Think about this: have you even been put into a better mood from reading something on the Internet? How about a worse mood? You never know the full effect of your actions, so try to make them have a positive effect.

For some, this idea of affecting the world becomes a bit overwhelming. You may think, "What if my good intentions

> *I feel like a better person for treating everyone like family. No matter what race or religion, everyone is a person and the same.* —Chris Wiegand

lead to some kind of bad effect?" Don't worry too much about that. Don't get a migraine from what one friend of mine calls "paralysis through analysis." If you do something positive, the outcome is out of your hands after that. We never know the exact long-range consequences of our actions or inaction, from the smallest to the biggest. However, it seems logical to believe that things you do out of compassion and giving have a much better shot at positive results than actions motivated by hostility or greed.

Please focus on how alike we all are. When you think about it, the sense of alienation that many people experience is largely circumstantial. Pick a random person on the street. If she were born in your body on your birthday, raised by your parents, and experienced the exact same things you experienced, she would be exactly like you. Imagine if you had been born into the life of a Buddhist monk, a Muslim scientist, a South American tribeswoman, or an Indian artist—assuming that you are not one of the aforementioned people. What makes you think that your actions and beliefs would be any different from theirs? Their world and experiences shaped them to the same degree that your world and experiences shaped you. Therefore, the differences among us are largely random chance.

— Idea —

Go out of your way to talk with people who seem to be different from you.

If you think in this way, you tend to develop a bit more understanding and patience. When someone clashes with your ideas or goals, this kind of thinking may help you to ponder how you would see the situation from his or her perspective. You may realize that you would probably think and act similarly to that person if the roles were reversed. You can ask yourself, "Would I have reacted any differently if I were in that position?" Maybe you'll decide that you would have. But at least you are thinking, and not merely reacting on impulses that can make things worse.

It puts things into a new framework when you begin to think this way. A new sense of connection begins to develop. One result is that you may begin to realize that the health and happiness of everyone is important. As I walk down the street, I often think about the lives of the people I pass—the little girl, the fireman, the fast food worker, the parking lot attendant. I sometimes make up names and stories for them in my head, and imagine their pains, joys, concerns, and triumphs. I make up a backstory for these random people (probably nothing like their real lives), and I try to think about

> *I have always found that treating others fairly does not only benefit them, but me as well. I always keep in mind that everyone has obstacles they are overcoming, and it has never benefited me to hold that against them.* —Brendon Schenecker

what kind of day they are having and why. I think about all of the things that we probably have in common. I know it sounds strange, and I chuckle at myself when I do it, but this kind of game leads to a sympathy and compassion for others that you would not believe.

People often begin dispensing unwanted advice with, "If I were you …" The truth is that, if you really were me, you would do exactly what I would do! That means you would make the same mistakes and have the same faults. Realizing this tends to make you a whole lot more tolerant of others.

Many people have heard of the concept of "six degrees of separation." It is the idea that everyone in the entire world, each of the six billion people, is connected through no more than six steps. If you took everyone you have ever met, everyone they have ever met, and so on, you will supposedly find that you need to go no more than six moves to connect yourself to anyone and everyone on the planet. This means that you probably have a friend who has a friend who has a friend who knows someone in a remote region of Australia. Get it? You are no more than six moves away from everyone else in the world, no matter how physically distant. You may have a friend or relative who works in the entertainment industry who has met a celebrity who has worked with relief efforts

— Idea —

Think of the last time a stranger annoyed you and list one reason why that person's actions may have been justified.

in a remote tribal area. If that is the case, you are separated from the celebrity by only two degrees and from the tribe members by only three.

This is a fun game to play, and it helps you to see that it truly is "a small world." If you start to feel that the world is too big and too complex for you to make a difference, this game can bring it down to size for you. You may want to play this game at a gathering. As the attendees start to think about who they know, and who those people know, it becomes apparent how quickly this net of connectedness develops. Before long, you realize that you are only four steps away from the Dali Lama, or the Pope, or the U.S. President, or the Prime Minister of India! Have you ever asked someone if he or she knows a good doctor / mechanic / dentist? This game is not much different, but you are establishing connections that you do not necessarily need (yet).

The idea of "degrees of separation" can also be used to network for businesses and charities. Some people say, "It's not what you know. It's who you know." That may be a bit of an overstatement, but don't underestimate the resources and connections of the people you deal with every day. I certainly would not discount the power of knowing your stuff, but let's at least admit that it is better to develop both what you know and who you know.

When you play the "six degrees of separation" game, you may find that it goes beyond mere entertainment, and even beyond enlightenment about the interconnectedness of all people. It may make your options and strategies open up and allow you to accomplish more by making new contacts. It may turn out that your new neighbor's second cousin is not only a senator, but a senator who is looking to start a new fund that could benefit your favorite charity. Perhaps an old friend never mentioned that her mother wants to open a café and will need someone to handle a service that you provide.

When I went to Chicago for the weekend, many people asked: "Why not stay at home in Pittsburgh and help people in your own city?" The answer was simple: "Why not help people in both places?" The point of the expedition was to show that we should care about everyone, not only those who happen to live down the block. Most people have a tendency to care about only those in their own communities. It is good to care about them, but why *only* them? I figured I could make more of a statement if I made a trip to all the way to Chi-Town to see what I could do there. Caring, compassion, sympathy, and goodwill are not limited resources like oil or gold! There should be plenty to go around. The news tends to make thoughts of limitation and bias even worse. Negativity in the news certainly attracts viewers and readers, but it may not always convey a great message.

A U.S. newsreader may announce: "A plane crashed in the Atlantic Ocean this morning, killing 212 ... including three Americans." I may be imagining this, but it seems as though the American death toll is like some kind of sick punch line: "Wait for it ... wait for it ...*three Americans!* Now it's getting serious! You have my attention!" What about the other 209? Why does no one seem to care about their fate? Are they somehow less important, less deserving to live? Surely their families and friends don't think so. I don't mean to be morbid here, but this is the best example I can think of to make this point. It is normal to care about those close to you, but there is enough goodwill to go around for everyone on the planet. The human family is like your personal family. You may not like everything they do or say, but they are your family, nevertheless. Everyone matters.

One of the first things you can do to improve the world is to change your thinking to include everyone in your thoughts, good wishes, concerns, and prayers. We are not talking about ripping down reasonable priorities. Everyone has a personal hierarchy of concern and loyalty. Most people put their family first (various people define family differently), and then their friends. After that, it may be their countrymen, or members of a club, or members of their religion. The point here is that you can also give a little bit of help to those who are not in your immediate circle. You probably spend most of your time in your hometown and with the same people. What if you spent one day of the year in another town or country? One weekend? Make an adventure of it! One day of the year is only .27397% of your time that year, less than one third of one percent. Yet you can accomplish so much in that time.

If your family is in need, of course you will take care of your family members first. If there is a crisis in your city, of course you will see what you can do there first. However, when things are going okay, why not send a package to an orphanage in another country? It is not too expensive to send packages internationally, although many folk seem to assume that it is.

We do not live in a bubble, and I would not want to. Your country has to co-exist with the rest of the world. This is one of the keys to improving the world: acknowledging that the rest of the world exists. It is time to focus on what we have in common instead of on our minor differences. Every single person on the planet, no matter how good or bad you think they are, was once a child with all of the innocence and potential of any other child. Does this mean that we should excuse atrocities? Of course not! It merely means that there is hope. The observation that the children and young adults of today become the leaders of tomorrow has become nearly a cliché. However, it is important to note this fact.

What effect must it have on children to think that no one cares, or that another country is hoarding all of the wealth of the world? Or that people from other cities or cultures have a bias against them? Let's look at the other side. How would it change a future leader's attitude about a foreign country if one of his or her fondest memories was that of receiving a toy from an anonymous person of that nation—sent just to show that someone cared? Would relations between these countries be a little bit friendlier? Who knows? It certainly seems plausible.

The more you travel or interact with people from around the world, the more you may notice how alike other cultures are to your own. One of my favorite experiences from my trip to Egypt, the best trip of my life so far, was when we exchanged stories and jokes with the locals one night. Once we caught on to a few key phrases and concepts, we found that their comedic thinking was just like ours. We sat all night among camels, gazing upon the Giza pyramids while our Egyptian friends made us laugh so hard we nearly wet ourselves.

Another interesting experience happened in Paris, at a coffee shop. I spoke very little French, and the people there spoke almost no English. However, with body language and genuinely friendly attitudes, we got to know each other and had a great time. There may be language barriers or differences in customs, but if you can manage to push past those, you will see that everyone wants pretty much the same thing: happiness. Call it cheesy, call it cliché, call it whatever the heck you want, but it's the God's honest truth. The tricky part comes when different people and cultures have conflicting ideas about what will make them happy, and about whether or not they care if anyone else is happy. However, if you help others to find happiness, it's only natural that you will find happiness of your own in the process.

> " *Teach students, not subjects. When people ask what I teach, I always reply that I teach students and then I explain this. The educational and practical applications are limitless and I could expound endlessly, but I have kids right now.*
> —*Joseph D. Deible* "

Providing an impoverished child with some cheap art supplies may allow him to develop a love of creating. This may encourage him to develop a productive hobby rather than getting into trouble. This may prevent him from engaging in criminal activity, and encourage him to become a constructive member of society. Far-fetched? Maybe, but probably not. Things like this happen.

Do you think it is possible that giving constructive options to kids anywhere could help them to avoid trouble and might possibly save their lives and the lives of others? You bet! Any suffering is tragic. If you can ease suffering in the world in any way, it will benefit someone. Who knows just how far your investment of time or money may go? You don't have to predict the future. You know that when you give from your heart, the positive feelings you get are truly worth the effort. We encounter thousands of situations a day. It is up to us to be aware that each has two potential outcomes: positive and negative. When you think about this, you have a better shot at making decisions that will cause each situation to have the best possible outcome.

Our connection to nature is also crucial. It seems as though many people have come to think of the natural world as something apart from them. If they bother to think of the natural

— Idea —

Ask the kids in your life what they would like to learn more than anything else. Then, do your best to get them started.

environment at all, it is something they think about as being a charity, a way to be nice if they get around to it: "I suppose I will be nice and recycle," or "I'm feeling generous, so I will donate to save a few pretty trees for the tree-huggers." Taking care of the environment is not a luxury, and it is not something that we should see as mere optional charity. It may be trite, but this really is the only planet we have. If you have a hard time conceptualizing environmental issues on a global level, then please think about the way that the destruction of nature can interfere with some of the best parts of your life, by destroying things that you may overlook: the trees that give you shade, the birds that sing for you, and the water that keeps you alive. I don't know about you, but I have always been a big fan of breathing clean air.

Shortsightedness about the health of planet Earth can lead to irreversible and catastrophic effects, the kind of effects that creep up on us. This is not a science book, and we are not here to debate ecological theory or policy. However, I would like to merely point out that the interconnectedness of all things certainly applies to the delicate relationships among all life forms on this planet. If you can understand how people can affect one another, it should not be difficult to see how we affect nature and nature affects us. Please try to figure that into your thinking as well.

Chapter Three
PRACTICE "PRACTICAL OPTIMISM"

You become like those people you allow to surround you. Pessimists have a tendency to mislabel themselves. They often say, "I'm not a pessimist. I'm a realist!" However, it is certainly possible to be unrealistically pessimistic. If you catch yourself saying or thinking, "This always goes wrong," or referring to "Murphy's law" ("Anything that can possibly go wrong probably will"), then you are starting to slip into the unrealistically pessimistic category. I don't know just who Murphy was, but I don't remember studying his so-called "law" alongside the works of Sir Isaac Newton. Yet people quote Murphy as though his ideas were as reliable as the laws of physics.

Just calling something a "law" does not mean that it is correct. People quote and misquote a lot of goofy or harmful statements as though they are true, apparently giving them credence just because they were written down somewhere (especially if they were written long ago). Many of the folks who say, "You can't believe everything you read" support pessimistic notions by quoting sarcastic sayings that they read on posters in gift shops or on signs at office desks. They choose to believe things that support their dysfunctional perspectives, even if it means quoting from silly sources. These types of folk rarely follow their own advice.

In some cases, misquotes comes from a simple misunderstanding of context. For instance, Solon stated, "Call no man happy until he is dead." This quote is taken out of context all the time. Solon was not saying that the dead are happier than the living, or that no one alive can be happy. According to various professors in the fields of Philosophy and Classical Literature, the intention of this statement was to point out that a person's life cannot be accurately assessed until it has been completed. He is saying that we should not come to a conclusion about whether a person's life was good or bad until we know how it ends. Pretty reasonable!

> " *Anyone can find error in anything if he or she looks hard enough. The point is to stop looking purposely for the negative and instead start living for the good that is always in front of us. —Jodi Matovich* "

Some tragic lives turn into magnificent triumphs, and some people who have every advantage die in misery. Just like in a marathon, part of the point is to finish strong. No one cares who led the pack for part of the time, or even most of the time. What matters is who crosses the finish line first. This is not to say that life has to be a race or a competition, but to make the analogy that even weary people can find the inner drive to blow by obstacles, especially when their goal is in sight.

Have you ever seen a film that moves slowly but builds up to an amazing climax? If you left the film early, you would not really be able to make a fair assessment of the movie's quality. How about watching a football game? Can you tell if it was a good game or a bad game, if you didn't watch the whole thing? If you are reading this, then you are still alive. If you are still alive, then your game is not over. Whatever you believe the score is now, you can still make a heck of a comeback!

Pessimists love to quote and misquote as though providing scientific evidence to support their hypothesis that their problems and shortcomings are the fault of God, the universe, bad

— Idea —

Think about something that you are dreading, and then write down five good things that can come from it if you approach it correctly. This can help you to learn to be positive about situations that would usually upset you.

luck, other people … anything but themselves. To think this way is harmful, inaccurate, and even humiliating. Who would prefer to think of themselves as powerless rather than admit their own mistakes and take massive actions to correct and improve? Apparently, a whole lot of people! If you are one of them, knock it off! It is not helping you! Does it make sense to quit at halftime?

Dealing with your negative thoughts is tricky, and there are geniuses out there who have done a much better job of explaining how to improve your thinking than I can accomplish here. However, I will give it a shot in the best way I know how. The most basic way to begin addressing your own little annoying "Downer Voice" is to ask what it has ever done for you. It's probably done very little.

There is a difference between your "Downer Voice" in your head and your "Practical Voice." The "Downer Voice" is a coward. It tries to avoid problems rather than tackling anything that could get in your way. The Downer Voice tells you, "It can't be done." The Practical Voice tells you, "We will do this, and we will do it right!" There is nothing wrong with acknowledging potential problems with your plan or goal. In fact, it is necessary. However, a potential problem does not mean that you should not try. Potential problems necessitate

> " *Sometimes things in life fall apart so that better things can fall together. —Stevie P.* "

planning and prevention, not abandoning your goal! Abandoning your goal because there will be obstacles is like refusing to try to score because an opponent will try to block you. Of course someone will try to block you! How much of a triumph would it be to score on an empty field or court? Overcoming obstacles is what makes it a triumph.

Millions and millions of people around the world have children every year, even though children create all kinds of potential problems. Just the pregnancy can be dangerous, but women put themselves through it all the time. Life becomes really interesting when the little guys learn how to walk! They get into everything. Countless problems come with having kids, but people who really want children don't let that stop them. They have an innate drive to share their lives with young people, and no problem is big enough to change that dream. If you are a parent, there is not much that life can throw at you that you haven't experienced already in some form: fear, doubt, frustration, hope, love, acceptance, and more.

When a child needs to learn something, how long do you try to teach that task before you give up trying? How long do you work on that goal? As long as it takes! You don't give up on your kid. I know I put my parents through hell (and they

---

— Idea —

Look at the "worst" things that ever happened to you and think about how crucial they have been in creating some of the "best" events.

have the grey hair to prove it), but they never gave up on me. Their devotion has made a world of difference. Whether you are a parent or not, make every dream a child of your creation, a sacred thing with a life of its own. Ensure your goal's growth in the same way that you would ensure a child's health and well-being. Protect your dream, nurture it, and enjoy every moment of its journey from infancy to maturity.

Now we get into the realm of thinking that I call *Practical Optimism*. The Impractical Optimists ignore problems. Practical Optimists address and deal with problems. Pessimists often look down on optimists because they assume that all optimists are Impractical Optimists. They do not understand the concept of Practical Optimism. Practical Optimists look at problems as temporary and manageable challenges that are necessary to overcome to achieve their goals. They want to be aware of obstacles, not to dwell on them but to eliminate them. For instance, Practical Optimists do not associate reasonable ignorance with negativity. No one can know everything. We pick and choose the knowledge that is important to us and try to update it as needed.

The most knowledgeable, wise people I have ever met tend to say two things pretty often: "I don't know" and "I was wrong"

> *I have worked day and night for months, even years, to get some things done, but accomplishing your goals is the best feeling in the world.* —Nate Carilli

(or some variation of these ideas). Don't be afraid to say you don't know something. Lack of information is usually an easy problem to fix. It shows you acknowledge your limitations and appreciate the knowledge of others. If you like, you may want to empower yourself by saying, "I don't know, but I sure am going to find out!" Or you may say, "I don't know anything about that, but it sounds fascinating! Tell me more!" That is how you learn. Don't be a "know- it-all." Become a "learn-it-all."

Similarly, if you find out you were wrong about something, you must have made progress to learn from the mistake. Smart people try not to make the same mistake twice. How can you discover you were wrong without having learned something that led you to that conclusion? Every "I was wrong" becomes a mark of progress when you think in this way.

Admitting ignorance or mistakes is often looked at as a negative experience. That is why pessimists do not seem to be as knowledgeable as Practical Optimists, at least in my experience. How can you put yourself in a position to learn as much as possible if you look at the gaining of knowledge as some kind of admission of inferiority? Many pessimists come off as "know-it-alls" because they look at the admission of their limitations in the same way they look at everything

— Idea —

Find someone who has a goal to accomplish something that you have done. Tell that person everything you can about what you learned in your own process.

else: negatively. They never admit error or ignorance, because they allow mistakes to make them feel foolish or powerless. It feels better to always act like an authority.

A pessimist's type of "free advice" can be the most costly advice you can follow. It may cost you opportunities, your health, even your friends. Good advice is a wonderful thing, but do not be cowed into following pessimistic advice just because the source seems to be certain or aggressive.

Enjoy learning, enjoy discovering, and enjoy diving out of your comfort zone and into new adventures of the mind. I've noticed that most students want to write papers about subjects they already know well. It is easier. I understand this, because school can be an overwhelming amount of work. Then there are others who seek out subjects about which they know nothing, just because they like to learn. They know writing that paper will be more work, but it's worth it to them. These students tend to be highly successful.

Everyone faces problems or obstacles to their goals. If goals were easy to achieve, we would all reach all of them in record time. A goal is a goal because it's hard. Otherwise, it would just be an average task. If you are fortunate enough to be entirely able-bodied, brushing your teeth is probably not a "goal." It's just something you do. If you have a limitation that keeps you

> *Not everyone is blessed enough to realize they need help.* —Kammi Plummer

from brushing your own teeth, and then you work for months in physical therapy to finally do it, then that is a triumph that's just as impressive as a Nobel Prize. *Success is not measured by where we are now, but by how far we have come.*

Practical Optimism does not mean ignoring problems or obstacles. It is the very process of overcoming problems and obstacles that makes your goals so impressive and your accomplishment of them such a triumph. I think that the key is to set a goal that inspires and challenges you; to acknowledge the problems in terms of what will have to be done; and then to move quickly on to planning the most efficient (and ethical) way to eliminate those problems.

Acknowledge the problems so that they can be tackled, but for no other reason. Consider that they are not even really "problems"—they are just necessary steps. Don't let the presence of obstacles deter you from accomplishing what you want to accomplish. Problems are speed bumps and detours, but not dead ends! Just know where they are and plan your route accordingly, without getting too upset. There is no reason to turn around and go home. Just check the traffic report ahead of time, fuel up, pack water and a sandwich, and get on the road with the best map you can create! (Forgive the extended road trip metaphor, but I think you see the point.)

— Idea —

Stop yourself the next time you start to push help on someone who does not want it.

Pessimists don't bother going anywhere, because there may be problems. They look at the locked car door as a problem, even though the key is in their pocket! Anything that is not effortless or convenient is a problem to them. Impractical optimists just jump in the car and hope for the best. Practical Optimists do a little bit of preparation and remain flexible to work around roadblocks without getting upset.

Keep in mind that there are many personality types. For instance, I like adventure, and I am very spontaneous. I plan quickly and wing it a lot. Other people feel more comfortable with a very structured plan. Figure out what works best for you and get started.

Problems or obstacles may be real—although sometimes they are not—but negativity is just an idea, a concept, or a way of perceiving. Negativity is the emotional baggage that comes with a perceived problem or obstacle. It does you no good at all, whether it comes from you or from someone else.

You can even learn to find opportunities hiding behind problems. I understand that the person who made "Post-it® Note Pads" was having difficulty creating an incredibly strong adhesive. Rather than simply discarding the weak adhesive he ended up with, he created a new application for it, and now millions (maybe billions) of people use "Post-it® Note Pads" all

Obstacles are things to be overcome. —Samuel Gridley Howe

the time. Now, that person is brilliant! Similarly, I have heard that the "40" in "WD-40®" is there because that formula was its creator's fortieth attempt to get it just right. What a wonderful testament to the power of determination to proudly place the "40" right there in the product name!

The only real failure is giving up on something you really want. Most successful businesses go bankrupt at some point. If you read the stories of some of the most successful people in the world, you will see that most of them (if not all of them) faced crushing "defeats" from which they eventually bounced back—stronger, wiser, and more determined than ever. If you learned something, it was not a failure. If you keep going after a major setback, that's a triumph in itself. It is a matter of training yourself for *solution-based thinking* rather than *problem-based thinking.* This is where Practical Optimism gets into specific, daily action.

Solution-based thinking can help on a daily basis. Let's say you have a problem like a leaking roof. That's annoying, to say the least. The problem is certainly not in your head (though it may be on your head). Anyone can see that there is a *condition that is not what you want.* To an extent, that is

---

— Idea —

List five factors that you see as obstacles in your life, and then write down how you would feel if you were to overcome those obstacles. You will probably realize that the joy of moving past obstacles will motivate you to take action.

all a problem is. Problems are only problems from a certain point of view. To the person who does roof repair for a living, your problem is a lucky break when business is slow. However, let's focus on your situation.

To you, a leaky roof in your home is a problem. Practical Optimism does not mean that you act as if it isn't happening, or dance around in the water, or wait for it to repair itself. It means that you go from acknowledging the problem to taking decisive action to solve it: solution-based thinking.

You don't throw a tantrum, you don't call to complain to someone about it, you don't obsess over how much it's going to cost before even seeing what is wrong. Ignoring problems just creates more problems. Obsessing over problems is probably even worse. Obsessing over the problem in this case means you went from having only a leaky roof to now having a leaky roof, high blood pressure, and relationship problems because you started blaming and yelling at everyone around you. After wasting all of that time, the roof leak has gotten worse, and now it will be even more expensive to repair all of the damage—so you have bigger financial problems as well!

I recently saw a TV show advertised about a famous person with a severe medical condition who tries to remain positive, no matter what. He made this show to get into the minds of

> *Gotta stay with it, because if you don't quit, it will eventually pay off.* —Michael (Tico) Hatala

other optimists, to see how they stay positive all the time. We could use more shows like this!

A person with a medical condition can be a perfect example of someone who is a Practical Optimist. For instance, I have the honor of being close friends with the great Dr. Jolie Bookspan, one of the most brilliant healers I have ever met. Jolie has overcome her own paralysis twice! Two different accidents paralyzed her, at two different times, and she made two full recoveries. She is the healthiest, most physically fit person I know, and she helps others to recover from a wide range of devastating physical injuries and conditions.

People have to understand their problems, address their problems, and then move beyond their problems. Failing to treat an illness can kill you, but so can obsessing over it. One of my friends was paralyzed in a very strange accident, a truly freak occurrence. He uses a wheelchair now, and does not have complete use of his arms. However, he is involved in more sports than I ever was! He knows exactly what he can do and exactly what he cannot do at this point, but he focuses on pushing the limits of possibility. He plays rugby and basketball, and has begun studying self-defense with me. He is wise enough to know that the life he has is worth milking for everything he can get out of it, and he is determined to test every limitation

— Idea —

Think about a time that you wanted to quit pursuing a goal, but you did not give up. What happened and why?

he perceives. An Impractical Optimist would probably not bother going to physical therapy because he thinks everything will just work out. A Practical Optimist who has been in an accident deals with the problem head-on, explores every possible option, and takes action!

Practical Optimism is based on solution-based thinking. You see the water leaking from the roof, put something under it to catch the drip, move possessions away from the wet areas, and explore the house to find the source—perhaps while talking on the phone headset with a friend who does repairs. You decide if you can fix it yourself. While doing these other things, you can try to think of anyone you know personally who does this kind of work—maybe even someone who owes you a favor! (So far, it has taken maybe five minutes.) If you can fix the roof yourself, you go to get the needed supplies. If not, you call around to get recommendations from trusted sources for the best rates possible. If it sounds expensive, you look into payment plans or ways to move funds around. You may even be able to talk to the repairperson and pick his or her brains about a business project, to see if you know some of the same people, or otherwise make useful contacts.

Practical Optimists usually like to learn, so you probably watch the repair, ask questions, and learn how to do it yourself if it comes up again. You got the roof fixed and a free lesson in home repairs so you never have to pay for that service again. Score! You just had quite a productive day! In other words, you think clearly, rationally, and wisely because you are focused on doing everything possible to remedy the problem as quickly, painlessly, and cheaply as possible, and on gaining every conceivable benefit from the situation.

If this concept sounds like common sense, then good for you! Seriously! However, you can probably attest to the fact that many people would spend all day freaking out, putting all their energy into blaming or complaining. Half the people I have met spend more time in freak-out mode than it would have taken to fix whatever it is that they are complaining about. We have all done that, and it is time to stop. Strive to be "cool, calm, and collected."

What about the negativity of others? That's a tough one. Maybe the negativity of others is best addressed in two categories: criticism and venting. Criticism is the harder to handle, because it is coming directly toward you. These are the situations when your dreams, goals, ideas, plans, or work are criticized or scorned "out-of-hand." We are not talking about helpful suggestions or truly constructive criticism. This negative criticism is the input that can influence you to feel foolish or hopeless.

The first thing you may want to do about criticism is to really look at the source. Does your critic have a high level of success in the field in question? Probably not. The most critical people in the world tend to be the least accomplished. It is a broad generalization, but check it out for yourself. Even those who tend to be highly accomplished in one field can be very critical in areas where they have no expertise. Who cares if your physician is not sure if your new business venture is a good idea? Who cares if your auto mechanic doesn't think you are taking the right medication? It's not that you should always ignore the opinions of others, but you probably know pointless negativity when you hear it. The main thing to remember is that it is usually not about you or about your idea or project. It is about the person giving you the feedback. The easiest test is to ask for suggestions. If someone can tell you what is "wrong" with your idea but cannot provide good alternatives, then there is no reason to get into a pointless debate.

Remember: Never ask a question if you don't want to hear the answer. If you truly are looking for opinions, don't get upset when people give them to you. Of course, they are not going to agree with you one hundred percent of the time. They are not you, so they are not as invested in your project. Additionally, others will always have a different perspective. Remember that you are the final judge when it comes to your own life. Listen, consider, and then decide if you should apply the advice or not. Someone just giving negative feedback, basing life on the "misery loves company" concept, should be recognized as such. Always examine the mindset of those trying to send

> " *I was the outcast, picked last for everything, made fun of for my style of dress, my haircut, etc. ... That changed quickly... but it taught me a valuable lesson that I will never forget. Racism, discrimination, jealousy, and prejudice are just plain old insecurity.*
> —*Scott Yoder* "

energy your way, and only allow input motivated by the best of intentions to even make it to your consideration phase.

In most cases, the opinions of negative people are more closely related to their own egos than to anything else. Someone who is jealous, wounded by a bad experience, or playing a self-serving angle will not provide you with sound advice. Listen first to yourself, and then to qualified, trustworthy experts who will focus on helping you. Listen to advice about how to make it happen, not about why you shouldn't even try.

If you have a new idea, someone will probably try to shoot it down. They may even be "looking out for you" in their own way, but this does not mean that you have to give up. One little test you can run is to ask them how they would feel if the idea went badly. If they launch into an emotionally charged rant about it, you know that this is about them and not you. Then ask them how they would feel if it went well for you, if the idea worked perfectly. Let them respond and listen closely. Then, go back to the question of whether or not it is a good idea. If they are turning this into something based on their feelings, then they are not giving you logical feedback.

People who are responding out of their own emotional needs—parents tend to be the worst at this—will not help

— Idea —

Think about an experience that made you re-evaluate another type of person. What made you realize that you were not being fair?

43

you to list pros and cons, making a reasonable decision about a new idea. They often operate out of fear of what will happen to you, and how they will feel if they "let it happen to you." Parents, other relatives, and friends, are looking out for your safety, not your success. Therefore, they usually don't like to hear of you taking risks.

This type of criticism gets especially tricky, because the people closest to you will be the ones who tend to have the strongest emotional reactions to your less conventional ideas. When it comes to your success and happiness, it doesn't really matter how they feel about your ideas. This is not to say that you don't care about their feelings overall, but their feelings about your projects should not keep you from going for what you want. After you reach your goals, you will be able to help them to gain the confidence to go after their own dreams.

People are usually terrified of the unknown, and change often leads to the realm of the unknown. Change is very intimidating for those who focus on problems rather than on possibilities. When you discuss a possible change, many people will become uncomfortable immediately, even if it does not affect them directly. Merely suggesting change in your own life

Instead of looking down upon people, look up to them. Your consciousness will be raised by default.
—Doreen Cameron

puts some people into defensive mode. There are many ways to communicate when it comes to this, and each case may be different. The main thing is that you politely "stick to your guns." If you don't think a certain person is at all receptive to your concept, don't bother asking for their opinion. Doing so would be a waste of everyone's time.

Rumors and gossip are another type of criticism. This kind of indirect criticism tends to be especially difficult to handle. Many of us have been guilty of spreading rumors at some point in our lives, even if the original intention was merely to tease. However, rumors are one of the worst kinds of negative criticism because they can affect so many people and get so widespread and distorted. At least you can defend your position and reputation when someone criticizes directly! Rumors are sneak attacks. You may not even know that the negativity exists until it has spread beyond control. If you tell people a secret, they will want to "scream it from the mountaintops."

One of my buddies in high school had a very embarrassing experience once. His girlfriend told one person, supposedly in confidence, and the entire school of 3,000 knew about it before our first class period. I wish that this were only a phenomenon

— Idea —

Stop yourself the next time you start to criticize someone else, and pay that person a compliment instead.

among kids, but it's not. You can tell a great deal about some-one's character by observing how that person keeps secrets and whether or not that person spreads rumors.

Some people have no interest in rumors, but they want to vent. They want to complain, gripe, whatever you prefer to call it. It is natural, when you are upset or worked up, to vent for a while. It is healthy to vent or to listen to venting, if it does not go overboard. If you have a disagreement with your spouse, you can vent to a friend about what is bothering you and get it out of your system. If your employer is driving you crazy, you can vent to your spouse or friend and end up laughing the whole thing off. The point of venting is to "let off steam" and give the negative feelings an outlet. However, once venting turns into obsessing over negativity, it can make problems worse.

It is common for people who need to talk to someone to begin stewing, working themselves into a frenzy by thinking about more reasons why they should be angry, depressed, or hurt. Listening to others vent is often part of a friendship, but there has to be a limit. It is natural to want to "get things off your chest," but we need to move on quickly from what we may generously call the "diagnosis" phase to the "cure"

I really don't struggle with the inner critic and such concepts. I'm a 'go-getter' and I don't bother thinking about failure because it affects the quality of my work if I do. —Eliz G. Tchakarian

phase. For those of us who are pretty direct and honest when dealing with our friends, we may say something like: "If you need to vent for a while, that's fine, but then let's talk about what you are going to do." This is a good way to start getting people to change their focus. If they start to come back around to venting, you can gently redirect: "I know, it sucks! Let's get back to planning what you can do so that you never have to deal with it again." By directing the attention to the solution rather than the problem, you have a shot at breaking the pattern of self-pity and negativity this person is experiencing, and getting the energy back to the real task at hand: making improvements.

Listening is very important and helpful, and it will be discussed more thoroughly later. However, it is good to think about that elusive line where listening becomes merely encouraging negative energy and pointless pessimism. It is not good for you or the person venting to just add to and encourage hostility or self-abuse. Spend a little time listening to a friend vent, then a lot of time listening to a friend brainstorm and strategize.

Practical Optimism makes sense for anyone who wants to accomplish anything. I know that the root of this idea is old and widespread, but I am hoping that reframing the discussion

— Idea —

The next time you find yourself criticizing someone's plan or dream, stop yourself. Re-focus and try to help your friend come up with ways to make it work.

may help a few readers to rediscover the reason and power behind this principle. Perhaps no one can be entirely happy and positive every second of every day. Just as physical pain is a necessary mechanism to communicate that all is not right with the body, mental discomfort is necessary to make us aware that something needs to be addressed.

Most people would not respond to the pain of a cut or scrape by rubbing lemon juice into the wound. However, millions of people do the mental equivalent of this by dwelling on things that make them unhappy rather than treating their psychological wounds. Does it make more sense to poke at your injury and ask others to rub salt into it, or to quickly and efficiently take care of it? Can you use your injuries as opportunities for learning and growth? Practical Optimism may not be easy, but it's a habit that can change your life.

A final word on Practical Optimism: Please keep in mind that Practical Optimism has nothing to do with aesthetic taste. Many subcultures develop an attitude of negativity and cynicism that they seem to think is necessary to be cool within their chosen groups. They think that a "Life sucks" or "I don't care" attitude makes them cool. Maybe it does. I don't know. I'm not a leading authority on being cool. However, please ask yourself this: Is it more important to be cool or to be happy? Maybe you can do both. It is up to you to decide what these words mean to you. But please don't make yourself miserable just to fit in with a certain group of miserable people.

One of the authors of this book made this mistake all through his teenage years. Being a Practical Optimist does not dictate your wardrobe, music collection, favorite films, books, or home décor. It is not necessarily reflected in your appearance or your hobbies. There is no "optimist's uniform," and no list of interests that are off-limits when you start thinking this way. You don't have to wear only colorful clothes and listen to happy music all the time. That's just a stereotype. You don't have to stop watching scary movies, wearing dark clothes, or listening to sad songs when you want to. The previously mentioned author would be in trouble if all of that were required!

Some of the most positive people I have ever met are self-labeled "Goths," "Punks," "Freaks," "Bikers," "Metal Heads," and members of various other subcultures that have been negatively represented because of unfair stereotypes. Practical Optimism has nothing to do with what you listen to, wear, watch, or read. We are not trying to change your style. In fact, we encourage you to express yourself in any way that works for you and harms no one else. Please do whatever keeps you happy and grateful for your life. We all have our interests, likes, and dislikes, and none of them preclude positive attitudes.

Practical Optimism is an option for everyone. It is a matter of simply embracing the life you love and helping others to do the same in whatever ways work for them.

Chapter Four

DEVELOP "WIN-WIN" THINKING

Some people look at the "win-win" situation as though it were a thing of folklore, a Yeti-like creature that has been rumored but not confirmed by science. There is a destructive lie that has people believing it is impossible to win without making someone else lose. That may be the case in certain sports or games where the rules are set up that way. But in "real life," we do not have nearly as many rules as most people seem to think we have. As long as you are not breaking the law or the rules of your religion, ethics, or morals, why not set the rest of the rules so that as many people as possible can benefit from every deal, transaction, project, and activity?

There are many ways to develop win-win thinking, including *practical, experiential, karmic,* and *emotional* win-win thinking.

Simply focus on everyone, including you, getting something that they need or want on some level.

Practical win-win situations result in everyone involved gaining something tangible, such as money, goods, or services. One way to do this is to dabble in bartering. Barter is great because it tends to focus on things that people already have in abundance, without involving currency. It is the oldest exchange system in the world. You trade goods or services for other goods or services of similar value. You can greatly enrich your life this way.

One way to get started in bartering is to make two lists: one of goods and services that you need or use on a regular basis, and another of goods and services that you can easily provide. Ask others to do the same, and then compare lists. You just started a barter network! You can exchange vegetables from your garden for babysitting, or help with a car transmission in exchange for custom-made boots. People who own land can allow people to camp there in exchange for whatever is needed or desired. You may even want to print up an official directory of the people you know, what they have to offer, and what they want.

The Web has created an entirely new world of bartering that is fast, efficient, and usually pretty safe (if the right precautions are taken). The Web is a great way to get the message out there when you want to barter. For instance, I have a friend who needed a cell phone—nothing fancy or even new, just one that worked. He placed an ad and exchanged a few e-mails. In no time, he found a guy who had just decided to upgrade his phone and still had the old one, which was in good condition. He needed to get his brakes fixed. My buddy had replaced brakes before, so that was no problem. Within a day or two, my friend had his phone, his new friend had new brakes, and they were both happy campers. The barter system is a great way to enrich your life and to develop win-win thinking.

Practical win-wins don't have to be based on barter only. There is nothing wrong with charging money for your goods or services. In fact, some customers would prefer the convenience of just giving you cash rather than time or goods. Money is not evil. It's just not the answer to everything. Cash works very well in certain ways. Many would agree that the key to win-wins with money is simply to approach the exchange ethically. If my friend had gotten a really good deal on the cell phone in a store rather than working on car brakes, he would have been reasonably happy with that as well.

Many successful business people agree that the important thing is to focus on giving more in value of goods or services than you receive in cash value. Just give people what you know is a good deal. They will be happy for the deal, and you will be happy for the return business and great word-of-mouth advertising. That too is a win-win. Many people get hung up on the quick buck, but that can come back to bite you. Not only is it unethical to overcharge or mislead customers, but it is bad for long-term business. Don't put yourself in the poor house or give things away for free all of the time, but figure out pricing that can make both you and the customer happy.

Experiential win-win situations add to professional and personal experiences in a valuable way. For instance, volunteering is a great way to develop your professional experience and credentials. Many people seem to assume that you must be paid for a job for it to "count." Do you think that someone who runs a large, charitable organization as a volunteer is any less a leader or manager that someone who gets paid to do a similar job somewhere else? If anything, the volunteer shows more dedication and character by doing the job without financial compensation.

On a professional level, volunteering can open doors you never would have imagined in terms of practical work experience, leadership experience, and contacts. Many of my friends have landed well-paying gigs as a result of volunteer experience, which almost brings the idea of professional experiential win-win thinking back into the realm of **practical** win-win thinking, just with a bit of a delay! Your volunteer experience builds your skills, your leadership, the way you handle stress, and the way that you communicate. All of these things will become incredibly valuable to you in one or more aspects of your professional life.

Personal experiential win-win thinking is one of the simplest and best approaches to giving; you do it for the simple experience

Go to work in a cheery mood and leave your problems at home. Then leave your work problems at work and always smile. —Debbie Julian

of it. This is a very important point for me. Most clichés are annoying and useless, but a few really stick with you. If "variety is the spice of life," then I want hot salsa running through my veins! You can call it a *"carpe diem"* attitude, a *"carpe noctum"* philosophy, or just a love of "bragging rights," but many of us just love variety in our lives and really enjoy doing things just to know and say that we have done them.

Personal experiential win-win thinking can be incredibly rewarding. Few things can make you feel more alive than doing something new, especially if you don't think you have it in you. Many of us keep extensive lists of our experiences, organized by whatever categories suit us. If you really want to have a good variety of experiences in your lifetime, if you are one of us who yearns to see it all and do it all, then please consider that helping others is a huge part of that. Challenge yourself!

> *"A smile is a facial expression that shows the warmth of the heart."* —Sherry Stehr

How many smiles can you spark in a day? How many people can you inspire? How many different charities can you help? How many kinds of people can you help? How many different

---

— Idea —

Develop a strategy to help you to separate your work life from your home life. It may be a slight change in your routine like changing into different clothes, or merely taking a deep breath when you cross the threshold.

---

kinds of animals can you help? Can you listen to someone and let that person inspire you? How many people can say they have helped to build someone a house, helped a total stranger, or talked with a homeless person over a meal? How many people can say they have paid a check for a stranger, helped someone to load groceries, or handed a wet person an extra umbrella?

One of the best things about doing something just for the experience of it is that it becomes a creative game. If you don't have the means to focus on doing huge things, you can get into the spirit of doing a huge variety of small good deeds, things that most people would never think of. When you do this, the experience is enough reward in itself. It is great to write these down and then look back at all of your adventures in giving. You may choose to keep them to yourself, or to share with certain friends who may be inspired by your ideas. Either way, every act of giving becomes a win-win situations when you think in terms of the experience you gain. You are your experiences. Build them, treasure them, and even record them. You may be amazed to see how much you can accomplish.

Karmic win-win situations revolve around the idea that good things come back to you. Practically every religion and philosophy in the world includes some variation of this concept.

> *I feel God gives me more than I deserve ... I believe in a God that gives us everything if we just work for him.* —Rahul Chovatia

Whether they call it "karma," "the three-fold law," or the "what goes around comes around" idea, most worldviews have some notion of cosmic justice. If this fits with your thinking in any way, then that should be reason enough for you to give all you can to others. A recent documentary included the story of a wonderful woman who donated a kidney to a stranger with no thought of reward whatsoever. A few years later, she won a major lottery, and continues to win smaller ones on a regular basis. She is convinced that her "luck" is a direct result of her good deeds, and I am in no position to disagree with her!

If you do believe in any sense of cosmic justice or balance, then it only makes sense to act on that belief by giving what you can to others with the faith that rewards will come to you in the way that they are meant to come. For those who believe in prayer, please consider this theory: God always answers prayers. Sometimes the answer is "Yes." Sometimes the answer is "no." Often, the answer is "wait."

If you act with an expectation of exactly how and when you will be rewarded by God or the universe, then the sincerity of your giving is in question. You are trying to barter with unseen powers. Barter with people, not with the universe. The universe does not work the same way as the human barter system. It

---

— Idea —

Ask friends to share stories of personal miracles, great events that came out of nowhere that they believe were gifts from the universe, God, or some other force.

gives to us without contracts or deals. It gives us life, energy, air, sustenance, and light without an agreement from us that we will give back. If you want karmic gifts from the universe or God, then give like the universe gives—naturally, freely, and without question—and the cycle will continue and expand. Give without a thought of exactly what you will receive in return, or when you will receive it. Just know that the rewards will be exactly what and when they should be. This is a matter of *faith*. If this thinking does not work for you, then please consult one of the other three types of win-win thinking and find your own motivation to contribute in a way that feels right.

Emotional win-win situations can be the most basic and powerful kind. Focus on the good that giving does for you emotionally. It is almost impossible to be sad when you have created joy. Giving may be the single best way to make yourself happier, and happiness is all that anyone really wants. What makes you really happy? Think of some things that cause you

> *The respect of another person's right to choose allows for a sincere decision to be made. If there is any kind of compassion or allegiance that is expected from another person, then there cannot be sincerity. Therefore, place no level of expectancy upon another person, and let that person choose freely. Not only pursue freedom for yourself, but allow it from others.* — Thomas Hasse

to smile uncontrollably. A hobby? A pet? A relative? How do you interact with these events, animals, or people? Positive interactions with your world are often reward enough for good deeds. Everyone is different, but many of us find that a child's smile, a senior citizen's wave, a cat's purr, or a dog's wagging tail may be well worth a little bit of effort. How about giving anonymously and observing the reaction? Like certain architecture or natural landscapes, joy and gratitude are often more beautiful when viewed from a distance.

How do you feel when you do something good? How do you feel when you know you have made a difference? This, more than any other subject discussed in this work, is up to your own self-exploration. There is not really much more to ask or say on this topic.

— Idea —

Try to keep in mind that compassion comes in many forms. Try not to assume that another person is "cold," "uncaring," or "selfish" because he or she does not communicate or act in a way that you feel is appropriate. Not everyone cries when sad, laughs when happy, or shouts when angry. We have the right to experience and express emotions in ways that work for us, so long as we try to avoid harming others.

Chapter Five

FOCUS ON BALANCE

Perhaps the same goofball who came up with the idea that someone always has to lose had something to do with the ridiculous notion that the pursuit of money forces you to live a life of selfishness and sin. I don't want to get into a religious debate here. You can decide what works best for you in that arena. Let's just leave it with the fact that money is a tool. Money is just like a hammer. It can be used to build a house for a person without shelter, or it can be used to bash in a window.

The question is not whether you should be rich or poor. The question is: "Are you a builder or a basher?" Are you going to use money to help yourself and others in healthy ways, or are you going to squander your money on self-indulgence? It is all about finding a balance. It makes no sense to collect a million hammers just to let them sit and rot in a barn, never being put to use. Likewise, it makes no sense to collect a million dollars just to let them sit and rot in a bank, never being put to use.

Sometimes wisdom comes in very small packages. Two of the most useful bits of wisdom I have ever encountered come in short sentences:

"You can't give what you don't have." —Dr. Wayne *Dyer*

"If you do what you've always done, you'll get what you've always gotten." —Anthony Robbins

The first line addresses a number of possibilities. It indicates that an empty vessel quenches no one's thirst. If you are broke, your options to help others become quite limited. If you are exhausted and have no time, your options diminish even more. If you are incapacitated, you are not much good to anyone. To help others, it helps to have resources. You need money, goods, time, and energy to be most effective in assisting others. It is not a new idea, but it is a good one. No one said you have to

> *Leave your personal problems at home and leave work at the office. When one is able to effectively do both of these things—most of the time balance and harmony can be achieved. Unless you've hit the lottery over the weekend...you might as well head to work on Monday and make it count for something!* —Lori Hughes

blow your money on a private jet. There is nothing wrong with having a jet, if it really suits your goals, but it is not necessary. Some say "The one who dies with the most toys wins." I say "The one who brings the most JOY wins."

Money works best when you use it to create more options for finding and sharing joy. Many people seem to believe that having money gives you FEWER options, which is ridiculous!

The Downer Voice says: "I'll be in the highest tax bracket and I'll have to pay half in taxes."

The Practical Voice says: "I would rather have half of a million than eighty percent of $30,000!"

The Downer Voice says: "I'll have to manage all that money."

The Practical Voice says: "I'll be able to afford good financial planners and accountants."

The Downer Voice says: "Everyone will bug me for money all the time."

The Practical Voice says: "I will have the ability to help those who need it."

The truth is that there is nothing wrong with making money. It's what you do with it that reflects on your character.

— Idea —

The next time you head in to work on a low-energy Monday, make it your goal to improve the day for someone else.

What you do with your money is up to you. Money is a vehicle that can take you various places. Money is not the destination itself. You can't eat money, or wear it, or shelter yourself with it. I suppose you could hypothetically TRY to do these things (you could tape a money suit to yourself if you really wanted to), but it would not work as well as trading the money for what you really want.

Sometimes I say things like: "I'm going to go trade this paper in my pocket for some coffee" just to remind myself that money is worth something only because we agree to treat it like it is. In reality, money is merely a symbol of potential changes in the world, from small ones to huge ones. When you buy a cup of tea, it moves from the shop's possession into yours. A tiny factor in the world has changed. When you spend money to buy supplies for hurricane victims to improve their lives, a pretty big factor in the world has changed. If you start to look at money as a symbol of potential changes in the world, then you may begin to re-focus your use of money in positive ways.

If you start thinking about using money to cause change to help others, it may alter your perspective a bit. Here is a little game to try: List everything that you would do to have fun if you had an extra $10,000,000. Next, make a list

I try to stay in a FANTASTIC state of mind, spreading smiles wherever I go. —Nick Mattiello

of everything you would do for others if you had another $10,000,000 at your disposal.

It is easy to get caught up in the joy of just how amazing it would be to have that kind of power. You could feed entire villages in poverty-stricken countries, set up new nonprofit organizations, build new animal shelters, or fund projects to end criminal activities like human trafficking and child abduction. Or, you could buy a private jet, a yacht, a fleet of luxury cars, and a country club for your own pleasure.

Which ones would you choose? What kind of person are you? How about spending some on yourself and some on others? Somehow the idea started circulating that money has to be all about you. There is no reason for that to always be the case. The point is to find a balance between the amount of money and possessions that you really need for yourself and the amount that you would gleefully give to worthwhile causes, including relatives, friends, people in your neighborhood, positive businesses, animal charities, international charities, environmental projects, and countless others.

I am not saying that you should not spend your money on things that make you happy. I am merely saying that it would be great if you explored a variety of ways that money can make you happy. Maybe split your excess spending between

— Idea —

Keep track of the number of times you can make people smile in a day. Try on a regular basis to beat your own numbers.

yourself and others. You may soon find that you get more joy out of the smiles of others than from the rev of yet another high-performance engine.

The stronger you are, the more people you can help. Don't deny yourself entirely. This is not a matter of meeting someone else's standards, but deciding and meeting your own. How much money is healthy and not greedy, according to your beliefs? At what point would material possessions become a burden rather than a blessing? How important is travel to you? How about designer clothes? Cars? There is no right or wrong answer, as long as you are being honest and true to yourself, not merely submitting to pressures and stereotypes that do not resonate in your own heart.

If designer clothes really make you happy, joyful, and grateful, then I hope you get everything you want. If you only buy them because you are worried about what others will say, I would gently encourage you to ignore the negative feedback of those who scrutinize. Focus on the only human being to whom you are entirely accountable: yourself. One of the writers of this book collects watches. The other one spends money on travel and does not even own a watch. Some of our friends are into buying art. Others buy computer equipment. There

> *I am who I am. I've always tried my best to find the confidence to say what I feel and do as I see right. It's the only way I really feel sane. —Nic Brooks*

is nothing wrong with using money for the things that help you to be happy. Your happiness will rub off on others, thus adding to the world's positive energy.

"Money does not buy happiness," but it can buy the things that help you to be happy, if you are in the right mindset. If you are determined to have a bad day, a new toy will not usually cheer you up for long. However, improving someone else's life and experiencing that person's joy and gratitude may do the trick. The key is balance. One strategy is to commit yourself to earning and keeping every bit of what you decide is healthy for you. Then commit yourself to giving every bit of what is left over to the people and causes that are important to you. If you give away all of your money now, then you become the one who needs help. You become a burden on others. If you invest your money, the investment earnings can help thousands of people, even after you are gone. Think about the lifestyle that is appropriate and healthy for you, and then consult a financial professional to help you to develop a plan that will benefit you and others.

Here's a story about a guy I know from some years back. Maybe ten years ago, money wasn't much of a factor for him. On a typical Friday night, you might have found him and his

---

— Idea —

Think of a situation in which you tend to feel shy or intimidated. The next time that situation comes up, state your opinion honestly but politely, no matter how nervous you are.

---

friends taking a limo out to the bars, running a $500+ tab, and calling it a night. "Great times," he was thinking to himself. "I am taking all of my friends out on the town, enjoying life, and living large." A few years of this lifestyle passed, and then he left the line of work he was in. No more six figures a year. It's a good thing he had saved some of that money, right? Wrong. He had spent every last penny living the "high life." How many people was he able to help then? He could no longer even do much to help himself.

A few years passed, and he started to save his money. He was a little older, a little bit wiser, but not much. On a typical Sunday, you could find him walking through the parking lot at the stadium, tailgating, and waiting for the Pittsburgh Steelers to bring home a win. He always took at least $60 cash, because he knew there would be people there who would need money: fundraisers for schools and charities, or individuals who were simply less fortunate. He now saved enough of his moderate income that he could give to a variety of people for a variety of causes and personal needs. When walking into the stadium right before the game, he would reach into his pocket and find pocket lint, nothing else. The $60 was gone in two hours

> *Thanks to the incredible support and love from my family, I've been able to overcome stress, grief, and loneliness. Every challenge we face gives us the ability to learn and grow.* —Krista Sibbet

or less. He did not even have enough left for a bottle of water, and his enjoyment of the game he had waited for all week was somewhat diminished.

This is no tragedy, but that is part of the point. He went from blowing big money and having fun all the time with no thought of the future to saving money to give away, but eventually feeling that he was poor and desperate. He helped out the charities and the less fortunate, but he also denied himself a "terrible towel" (Steelers fans know what I am talking about) or a pretzel at the game. These are little things, but sometimes the little things keep up our spirits and help us get through the day. He had not yet learned to give to others and himself in a balanced way. He realized that he did not want to squander his money on things that were "unnecessary," but some things that are not necessary to basic survival are really necessary for your morale. They are rewards for your hard work.

If you work 16 hours a day and don't have much relaxation time, it's okay to purchase an "unnecessary" boat, a car, new electronic equipment, or a trip to reward yourself for all of your hard work. That keeps the balance in your life as well.

— Idea —

Think of a specific challenge that a family member or friend helped you to overcome. Write a note of thanks to that person, relating specific details to demonstrate how well you remember. Do this even if the event was long ago, or if the person is no longer alive.

The system becomes unbalanced when you take too much or give too much.

Too much of anything is bad. Aristotle used to say: "The happy man is he who seeks the middle way." If you eat too much of anything, your body will let you know through signs and symptoms. You can't drink too much water. Your system will not let you keep what you can't handle. Even healthy things can theoretically make you sick if you ingest too much. That works for your mind as well, especially when it comes to money. Your unconscious mind will not allow you to have more money than it believes you can handle or deserve.

Don't feel guilty about receiving material things for the services you provide and keeping a reasonable portion for yourself. You are denying yourself the pleasures of life if you give it all away, and this may lead to depression, resentment, and a number of other mental effects that can harm you and make you less capable of helping yourself or anyone else.

The second quote that I mentioned a while back—"If you do what you have always done, you will get what you have always gotten"—is also very important. Simply trying new things might improve your situation and performance. This is not a business manual, so we are not here to dispense moneymaking advice. We will simply urge you to look into new options if

> " *Those who whine don't win. Those who win don't have time to whine.* —Perry Coleman "

you are not happy with your current state of being. Look to the experts for ways to change what is not working.

So many people bang away at their lives with determination, but no Practical Imagination. They seem to think that unwavering persistence alone will somehow miraculously revolutionize their lives one day. Maybe, but I doubt it. Why throw yourself against a wall when the door is wide open for you to walk through? If you are unhappy with your finances, health, relationships, contributions, or results, then it means that you are out of balance in some way. You will need to do something different to get different results. To believe otherwise is to set yourself up for misery and stagnation, or mediocrity at best. Don't leap into something blindly just because it is new, but think about every possible option for finding a new balance. Be willing to experiment and see what works.

— Idea —

Don't talk about what you are going to do all of the time. Try accomplishing something without telling anyone what you intend to do. Then, share the good news after it is done.

Chapter Six
LISTEN TO OTHERS

L istening is one of the most important things you can do to improve your life and the lives of others. Unfortunately, it is a rare and under-developed skill these days. There are several reasons why listening is so important. Lack of communication is usually the greatest problem in relationships, the workplace, schools, and in global diplomacy. This may be because most people associate communication only with sending out clear messages. Receiving and processing information is fifty percent of communication. It is not enough to say what you have to say. That kind of thinking is what leads to people merely shouting over each other. Perhaps this is the main difference between a discussion and a fight. A discussion should be an open exchange of ideas in a give-and-take relationship, whereas a fight degenerates into a situation where everyone is yelling and no one is listening. If you do not understand someone's point, or someone confuses you, it is usually at least partially your fault for not listening or asking questions.

Part of the listening problem today may come from social anxiety. According to various polls, public speaking is the most common fear in America, more so than death! This may be why people obsessively plan their own words and tune out what is being said. This problem arises in most conversations within the first few seconds. How often have we forgotten someone's name immediately after being introduced? This is probably because we were obsessing over how to present ourselves. We may be terrified of embarrassment, or planning the best strategy to make a good impression. The irony is that immediately forgetting a name that was just told to you may seem sillier than stuttering a bit!

We can all begin today to be better listeners by simply concentrating on what is being said. We have been talking and expressing ourselves for our entire lives. Some may have more natural speaking talent than others, but most of us can pull it off pretty effectively. Let us move on and focus on being good listeners, and trust that the words will come to us. There are

> *Once you know someone's fear you know every-thing there is to know about how to love them and hurt them; it's these brutal truths that bond people for life.* —Amy Hartman

many smooth talkers out there. If you really want to impress someone, show that you have listened carefully.

Listening lessens conflict. Many conflicts begin because of misinterpretations due to poor listening. If you listen closely to what is actually said, you may find that input that seems insulting or negative was not really meant that way at all. Sometimes it helps to ask for clarification. When someone says something that sounds rude or inflammatory, you can politely ask that person to clarify. If you say, "I know you didn't just call me stupid!" then you are just looking for a fight. Perhaps instead you could ask, "So what do you think that means?" or "What would you recommend?" or simply say, "I'm sorry. I did not quite catch your meaning." You may find that those who seem to be insulting you or trying to argue are just not terribly eloquent, and that they did not mean anything negative at all. If you go into a conversation looking for a fight, you will probably force one to happen—but what have you gained from that?

Listening communicates compassion. Simply listening with attention is one of the best ways to let someone know that you care. You don't have to fix things, and you don't have to give advice. Just really listen and show interest in the speaker's

— Idea —

List a way that one of your fears holds you back from living the life you want. Next, list three things you can do to move past that fear. Do those three things.

wellbeing. Half the time, people just want to express themselves, and it is not usually considered appropriate to talk to stuffed animals, trees, or walls. They need an audience. If another person listens, the speaker often works out problems or feelings in the process of explaining or expressing. Your job as a listener is to pay attention, show interest, and respond minimally and positively. Do not feel obligated to solve a problem, but do not withhold valuable information if you think it really can help! I don't know how many people I have met who continue to offer me amazing kindness, consideration, and direct help, simply because I listened intently and with sincere interest to them the first time we met.

As I mentioned previously, one exception to this concept of listening to others express themselves comes up when the speaker is merely venting for a long time, dwelling on negativity. Too much venting is unhealthy for both of you, so you have the right to save yourself from infectious negativity by redirecting the conversation a bit and helping the person in question to switch gears into constructive thinking rather than destructive thinking.

> *I think as many of us get life experiences, we do know enough to make a difference. But many of us choose to not care enough. True change cannot happen unless you care enough. And if you do, you can change the world.* —Kerry Taylor

I don't know about you, but I can listen to positive people all day. However, negative talk is draining, pointless, and unhealthy. I think that good friends listen, understand, support, and encourage. Don't add to the negative emotion, and please do not get into "one-upsmanship" about whose life is more miserable! That is even more destructive than merely listening to an hour of complaining. It escalates the negativity to new heights of destructive power. When someone is having a hard time, please show sympathy, caring, and understanding by listening. Then ask questions that help to direct him or her into a more positive state of mind, without rattling off unsolicited advice or platitudes. This can work wonders.

Listening allows you to learn more. I am routinely asked by my students how in the world I learned all of the information I rattle off to them. I mention this not as a matter of arrogance, but as a specific and useful example of why listening is so important. I tell them the two most important tricks I know to learning, and I will tell you now.

The first trick is to change your perspective to a learning perspective. Just about anyone would probably agree with the observation that people tend to remember things that

— Idea —

Think of a cause or group that makes you feel deep sympathy and compassion (children, animals, the elderly, victims of crime, the poor). Get involved or contribute to that cause in some way ...today.

77

interest them. For decades, parents have been asking kids, "Why can you remember every song lyric on the radio, every character on your TV shows, and all of the personal information about every one of your friends, but you can't remember enough to pass a chemistry test?" The answer, of course, is obvious. They actually care about certain information, and they cannot bring themselves to be interested in other information. What does this tell us? It tells us that memory is, at least partially, a state of mind and a function of perspective—and that perspective is a matter of choice. It can be changed almost instantly.

Here is a game that I play with my students. You may like it. I ask someone to select a random physical object in the room. It may be a pencil, a piece of chalk, a book, or anything else. I then ask this rather overwhelming question: "In order to understand everything that there is to understand about this one specific item (this particular one, not an item like it), what would we have to understand?" They begin usually with its basic physical properties, and I begin recording on the blackboard. They may say that we need to know its dimensions, materials, color, and weight. Then they usually move on to slightly more abstract things that we would need to

> " *I was often afraid to look a stranger in the eye or say hello. So I quit watching the news.* —Heath Curran "

understand: its uses, its inventor, where it was manufactured, who has used it, how much it costs.

I then help them to move onward. To understand color, we must understand color theory, art theory, the neurobiology of the visual process, optics, and physics. In order to understand the item's measurements, we need to understand the history of measurements, English and metric systems of measurement, the nature of numbers, mathematics, and the tools of measuring. In order to understand the object's inventors and users, we would have to learn the biographies of every single person who ever touched, used, or thought of anything like it, as well as their anatomy, physiology, and psychology as humans (presumably the only species to use that object on a regular basis). The exercise goes on and on until the board is covered from top to bottom, and the students are beginning to catch on to the notion that we are just warming up.

What is the point of all this? There are a couple of them. One point is to demonstrate that, in order to understand everything there is to know about any one thing, you have to understand everything there is to know about everything. The students react differently to this. Some of them say, "So what's the point of studying anything if you will never know it all?" Others see where I am going with it as I explain that another approach is to see that everything is interconnected (as discussed previously with regard to people).

I explain to them, "We ended up having the great American genius George Washington Carver on this side of the board, and one of your favorite video games on the other side. If nothing else, we have managed to demonstrate that they at least have Dave's cell phone in common in some way!" The "six degrees of separation game" works with ideas and objects just like it does with people, but it tends to be even easier.

This leads to the next point: If you focus on the interconnectedness of everything, subjects that once seemed boring start to be relatable to subjects that fascinate you. When you can relate everything to something that fascinates you or helps you, everything becomes more interesting. When everything becomes more interesting, everything sticks in your memory a bit better.

Once you learn the trick of seeing everything as being connected, you can learn the next trick, which is applying everything to yourself, your life, and your personal interests. When everything seems connected, then everything becomes more personal. You can see how anything you encounter can help you to understand and appreciate your life, interests, and goals. Kids who saw chemistry as boring may start to think about the chemistry in the materials in their skateboards or video games. Tedious tasks at work may become easier to keep

> *With age, I've realized that my greatest failures led me to my greatest triumphs. If I can analyze my failure and learn something from it, it wasn't a failure at all. —Anonymous*

straight as you consider how vital they are to keeping the whole operation running smoothly.

One of the best ways to really capitalize on this newfound perspective is to focus on your listening skills. Now you can listen to everything and learn more because you can apply so much of what you hear to ideas that already fascinate you and add to your life. Keep those "feelers" out there. Everyone has something to teach you. Listen actively, probing for connections and positive uses for the information that is communicated.

In a short conversation, you can learn as much from a child as an adult, as much from a homeless person as from a professor, and as much from a senior citizen as from a physician in her prime. It just may not be what you originally had in mind to learn. That's okay. Be open to all learning, going in without preconceived notions about what will result. Go into every conversation thinking, "I don't know what I will learn, but I am sure I will learn something fascinating!" Listen closely and enjoy applying your new knowledge in ways that help you and those around you.

Listening allows you to help more efficiently. Finally, listening helps you to help others. It seems as though many people want to help— even insist upon helping—but already have it set in their minds exactly how they want to help. If it is really about the person you are helping, and not just about yourself, you need to begin by listening.

Someone who desperately needs an air conditioner to avoid heat exhaustion is not going to benefit much from you bringing over a bunch of blankets, no matter how nice the blankets are. A vegetarian may thank you politely, but that does not mean that he is actually going to eat the thirty-four cans of chili you dropped off. Most people will be grateful that you helped, no matter what you do; it is always nice to know that someone cares enough to act. Is that really enough for you? Do you merely want to collect your "Brownie points" for a misguided, halfhearted attempt, or do you actually want to change the world, at least in some small way? If you have made it this far through this book, I will guess that you chose Door Number Two. The most efficient ways to help usually involve listening first.

Listening does not mean that you have to do exactly what is asked or suggested. If someone who is dying of liver disease asks you to pick up a bottle of vodka, you certainly have the right to inquire about any other needs you may be able to meet. If you cannot provide one thing, you can certainly ask if the

> "Not everyone is the same. To be judgmental because someone is overweight, gay, practices a certain religion, etc. ... is just plain ignorance. It's almost a guarantee that everybody has some characteristic or 'flaw' that is not going to agree with everybody out there. These people need to get over it (and themselves) and just accept that not everyone is made the same, and think of better things to do with their time than break down others. —Joe Walsh"

people in question have any need for certain other items that you have available.

Many people say, "They should be grateful for anything they get." This is true to an extent, but we are not talking about their level of gratitude here. We are talking about your role in making a real difference in the world. It is a practical matter of getting the right help to the ones who need it.

Listening helps to get things done right. Whether the problems are at work, in the family, at school, or even on a political level, listening has the potential to bring up new solutions. Solutions develop when everyone involved finds a balance between speaking and listening. Try to listen for the strengths, contributions, and ideas of others. Focus on how to capitalize on the strengths and ideas of others, rather than overruling or controlling them. Ask yourself: Is this about your ego, or about accomplishing the goal? Once you decide this, you can move forward.

Sometimes, people don't know exactly what they need to better their lives. They know the end result they are looking for, but they are not sure how to get there. If you listen closely,

— Idea —

Think of a type of person who tends to make you uncomfortable because of your own assumptions or biases about race, religion, nationality, profession, lifestyle, subculture, etc. Be honest with yourself. Try to have an in-depth conversation with a member of that group, focusing on that person's positive qualities.

ask questions, and really think about their situations, you may be able to experience the joy of being a true advisor—and not just another person with an opinion.

I don't know about you, but I find myself talking and interrupting all the time, especially when I am really excited about something. It is much better to listen more, letting others finish their thoughts so that you can communicate better. This sometimes backfires when people jabber on for hours, but you can find a balance between talking and listening.

From now on, try to really listen when you meet someone. This is tougher than it seems at first. You don't need to plan your greeting in your head. You greet people all the time. It's really not that stressful. You know your own name, but you don't know this new person's name. Repeat their name back and then use it a few times throughout the conversation. This helps your listening skills and memory, and it also makes a good impression.

If there is someone whose name you should remember—but you don't—be honest: "I am so sorry. I am trying to improve my memory for names. I always enjoy talking with you, but I have not heard your name for so long. If you tell me again, I will remember from now on." Then, of course, you have to live up to your promise.

Many people say that "knowledge is power." Let us empower ourselves by listening and taking in all of the knowledge that others want to share. Let us gratefully receive knowledge from people from all walks of life, and from nature as well. Let us listen to the input of people from different professions.

The scientist, the waitress, the truck driver, the dancer, the artist, and fireman all have things to teach us. Every legitimate profession adds value to our world, and all are noble. They all bring different types of good into the world. So please do not judge the profession of another because you do not recognize the good that it does.

If you do not understand the value of a profession or a major, you can politely ask people in that field what drew them to it. When you listen to the passion and wisdom that comes through, you may choose to spend more of your time listening to what they have to say about the way that their fields interconnect with others. Rather than asking "What in the world are you going to do with that degree?!" perhaps you could ask something like: "What drew you to that program? What kind of a career would you like to have?" Think about what the world would be like if no one did that job. Then listen. You may find that "frivolous" or "pointless" majors or jobs are not so silly after all.

Chapter Seven

ENJOY GIVING AND RECEIVING

iving to others is one of the best things that you can do for your health, your mind, and your happiness. Everyone has something to give. Every single person on the planet has something to contribute to the world, and few things make us feel more needed, more valuable, more useful, and more respectable than giving to others. Everyone has the opportunity to give **money, time, knowledge**, and **care**. Once you explore all of the resources available to you, you will see how rich you truly are. As I said before, you are a powerhouse for positive change!

Whether you have begun to fully use those resources or not doesn't matter. What are you going to do now?

Money: Some people have quite a lot of money to give. Oprah Winfrey, Warren Buffet, Bill Gates, Montel Williams,

Anthony Robbins, Ellen Degeneres, Ted Turner, Sir Richard Branson, Michael J. Fox (in no particular order), and countless other wealthy people donate millions of dollars to worthy causes each year (sorry to the many others who should have been listed here—we appreciate you all). However, not everyone has millions to contribute. How about thousands? Hundreds? Tens? If each person just in the United States donated an extra buck or two, we would have hundreds of millions of dollars more for good works ... and millions of Americans and others around the world do donate money to worthwhile causes every single year.

Many people ask, "How do I know that the money is getting to the right place?" Well, how do you know that the money you pay for lunch is getting to the right place? The cashier could be skimming from the till! Maybe the cash will not be claimed on the business owner's taxes. Is that really your job, to trace these things? I doubt it. Your job is to do what you know is right according to your own moral and ethical code. Other people have to do the same. Once money passes into someone else's hands, it is someone else's money and someone else's responsibility.

Of course, I would encourage anyone to check into the charities you support. It would be ludicrous to say that you should not care which charities are the most reliable and ethical. My point is merely that you should not let paranoia about how the money is used keep you from giving. If you are not sure about how much of your dollar goes to a certain charity, then find a charity that you do trust and give to that one. You may want to check out some local "grass roots" organizations where you can talk directly with those who control the finances. Some people use the question of the organizations' use of money as an excuse to give nothing. That type of thinking is not healthy or charitable.

Time: Time is a resource. You are here for only so long. What will you do with your time? Will you squander your time on mere self-indulgence, or will you balance your time between productive work and relaxation, helping yourself and helping others? I don't know about you, but when I am honest with myself, I have to admit that I am much more stingy with my time than I am with my money. I haven't cut my own grass for years. It's not because I'm lazy or unable to do it. It's because enjoying my days off is worth $25 to me. Just as different people have different amounts of money they are willing to contribute, they also have different amounts of time to contribute.

When you start to look at your time as a resource (and people who are terminally ill would agree that it is your most valuable resource), you may start to think about investing your time as wisely as you know you should invest your money. You may want to set aside time just for charitable deeds, or you may want these deeds to be more spontaneous. You may be able to donate one day a week, one hour a week, or maybe only ten minutes per week. Whatever time you have, we have ideas toward the end of this book that can help you to use those precious minutes to do something you can be happy about.

One of the most valuable concepts taught by several success theorists is that of the power of a moment. Think about how many major changes can happen in a few seconds. It only takes seconds to accept an offer, to reject a deal, to say "I do," to say "Let's do it," to hit the brakes, to pull a trigger, to dial "911," to step onto a plane, to hit the "enter" button on a computer, to be pronounced guilty or innocent, to be pronounced a citizen, to sign a contract, and to do millions of other things—for good or ill. Please think about some of the split seconds that changed your life. Now think about split second events that you could create that could change the lives of other people, animals, or the natural environment.

Knowledge: The phrase "knowledge is power" is thrown around quite a bit these days, but I doubt that many people really think much about what that means. Yes, it is good to know things, but acting upon knowledge is what changes the world. Knowledge does not do much good when it is just sitting in your head. Everyone knows things, and everyone over a certain age probably knows things that can be quite useful. Consider the types and levels of knowledge-power that you wield, and think about them from an outsider's point of view.

You may not have thought about the value of your knowledge because it has become commonplace in your life, "old hat." However, if you consider why you learned it, how you use it, and how others could use it, you may see that your knowledge

> *On any given day, the more you do, the more time you end up having!* —Gina Mucciolo

is a goldmine of possibility. What do you do for a living, for a hobby, to get through the day? Does anyone else do those things? Probably. Does anyone else want to do those things one day? Probably. The job that you complain about would be a dream job for someone else. You can spend a little bit of time teaching people what you have learned about that field. The household chores that you could do in your sleep are an enigma to anyone who has not learned about them. Why not teach a youngster (your kid or someone else's) how to do dishes, do laundry, replace light bulbs, run a vacuum cleaner?

No matter what you know, someone else wants to know it too. Do you have a hobby? I can almost guarantee that someone in the world is just starting to get into it and would love to have your advice. There are many ways to make a gift of your knowledge: writing books / articles / Web logs / e-mails, holding small classes, doing seminars at libraries or schools, and offering private tutoring. There is nothing wrong with charging money for your services—as long as your rates are reasonable—but I would urge you to donate your knowledge regularly.

Care: In addition to money, time, and knowledge, there is also the gift of caring. Even if you feel that you have no money,

---

— Idea —

Experiment with new ways to use your time effectively: new planners, organizers, schedules, safe multi-tasking, group work, etc.

---

time, or knowledge to contribute—highly doubtful, but we will go with it hypothetically—merely showing care is enough to change the world at least a little bit. For instance, I was having a bit of a downer day a while back, and the person who took my order for my BLT on a bagel at my local sandwich shop changed my whole day, effectively changing a tiny segment of my life. She smiled and demonstrated sincere friendliness and care. She seemed to just be acting in her usual cheerful way. It was not the first time I had seen her, and there was not anything really unique about her behavior. But, when she asked how my day was going, she seemed like she really wanted to know. When she said to "Have a great day," it seemed like it really meant something to her. She really seemed to care. I don't know why I thought this, but her actions hit me just right on just the right day, and a potentially terrible day turned out to be a great one. I doubt if she has any idea of her impact on me. The really funny thing is that I don't remember what had me so bummed out that day, but I distinctly remember her and how much better her kind words made me feel. When you focus on the caring, the problems seem to fade away.

" *I survived by the guts of my only friend ... If not for Peter's bravery and caring, I would not be alive today. I was abused and told I would never amount to anything ... I have had to prove a lot of people wrong.* —Charles Patterson, "Staypuff" "

If you are not convinced that showing care can change the world, consider the life-saving smile that never happened. Caring can literally save lives. You may have heard of the study that was done regarding suicides on the Golden Gate Bridge. In one case, the person in question wrote in his note that he was going to go to the bridge to jump off. He claimed that if only one person smiled at him on the way there, or showed him any human kindness, that he would not kill himself. Apparently, no one felt like mustering up the energy to crack a smile at this lonely soul, and he is no longer with us. This is possibly the most tragic story I have ever heard. One second and a few calories of energy in the facial muscles from anyone he passed could have saved his life. Why don't we consider that anyone we pass could be "walking to the bridge"?

Everyone you see on the street has a different story. The "tough looking" kid, who you may think is a "hoodlum" or "thug," may have just found out that his mother is very sick. The "mean looking" lady could merely be worried because she just lost her job. It is so easy to slip into judgmental thinking about people we don't even know, but we can also develop a perspective through which we see every single person as a former child who has had to face fears, disappointments, heartbreak, and regret. Every single person you meet could tell you a story that

— Idea —

Name one person who stood by you during one of the worst times of your life. Thank that person.

would make you want to cry. Every single person you meet could tell you a story that would make you want to cheer. Will you give them a chance? Will you put forth the effort to show a smile, a wave, or a pleasant greeting—whether you think it will be returned or not?

Now, let us look at a story of caring. On the other end of the spectrum of stories there is the man who set out to spread cheer and goodwill by offering hugs to strangers. At first, many people thought he was crazy or up to something. Eventually, it became a phenomenon. People from all walks of life were greeting and hugging around him like family. His Internet video has led to re-creations of this event.

The simplest acts are often the most powerful. Are you thinking what I'm thinking? If the poor man who leapt from the Golden Gate Bridge had encountered the kind gentleman giving free hugs, the world would probably have one less suicide and the joy of a transformed life. Energy is infectious, whether

> *Give without remembering and receive without forgetting. —Author unknown*

— Idea —

Simply consider this quote, and try to live by it. We will do the same.

it is positive or negative. So why be part of the problem when you can be part of the solution?

You can also show you care for others by allowing yourself to receive from them. "It is better to give than to receive" is another saying that tends to set up dysfunctional thinking in the minds of many. Giving is every single bit as important as receiving, but it is not necessarily better in an absolute sense. If you refuse to receive, you deny people the joy of giving. Giving can be the most joyous, fulfilling thing in the world, so why would you want to take that away from someone? Sometimes it's a matter of pride. Other times, it's a matter of guilt. Neither of these thought patterns are terribly useful. On my birthday, I almost feel awkward receiving gifts. This seems to be a pretty common reaction. When I think about it, I realize it's not about the gift or even about me anymore. It's about the happiness of the person who enjoys giving and seeing my gratitude.

Show you care by accepting someone's help, even if you don't need it. You may not feel that you need to receive, but they may experience a strong need to give to someone in order to lift themselves up. Accept their help, whether you need it or not. Then, show true gratitude that this person would go to such trouble. Give warm thanks. It's not about how they helped you. It's the fact that they *wanted* to help you that should make you grateful. This person chose you to assist in that moment, out of all of the people on the planet. What a gift!

When you start to think in this way, the receiving is actually not about you anymore. You are not really receiving so much as giving the joy of giving! Receiving is absolutely necessary to giving. You have to receive something to pass it on, and someone has to be willing to receive in order for you to give. Be open to receiving all of the good things that people, nature, the universe, or God have to offer you. You don't have to keep them, but you can receive them, enjoy them, and then pass them along. Whether it's a dollar, a favor, or a smile, you usually have to receive it from someone before you can "pay it forward."

> *If we succeeded at everything on the first try, we'd never learn the lessons that adversity teaches us. Things that come too easily are not appreciated. And it's an insult to our Creator when we give up. We were given an amazing ability to survive and strive. It's up to us to do the best with that ability.*
> —*Jimmy Roach*

— Idea —

Write down what you learned from an experience that seemed to be a failure.

Chapter Eight

EXPLORE YOUR OPTIONS THROUGH "PRACTICAL IMAGINATION"

s I said before, there are many excellent books out there that are much more in-depth when it comes to exploring the best mental approaches to giving. However, I figured that it could not hurt to review a few classic ideas from a slightly different angle. Different people have different learning styles. If this book "clicks" with just one person in a way that other books have not, then it was worth the effort.

At this point, I would like to go into my best use of Practical Imagination. The following is a set of lists of specific actions that you can take to improve your world. Similar projects have presented similar lists, but we believe that this one is especially imaginative, practical, and extensive. Furthermore, it is organized by your investment of time and money.

As previously discussed, many people do not believe that they have the time or money to change the world, or "win some victory for humanity" (Mann). The following list of suggestions (and that's all they are) is broken down into actions that require one minute or less, five minutes or less, ten minutes or less, one hour or less, two hours or less, and one day or less. It then brings in factors of money: $1 or less, $5 or less, $10 or less, $100 or less. Our goal here is to provide so many action options, with so much flexibility, that you can look at changing the world as an everyday activity, like eating breakfast or getting ready for bed.

Some of these options focus on you. Remember that you are a part of the world, so changing yourself is one of the most fundamental, crucial, and practical parts of changing the world!

How you use the list of contribution ideas at the end of this book, like most things in your life, is entirely up to you. If you want to use it, use it in the way that works best for you. If you don't want to use it at all, maybe you can at least pass it on to someone else who may make use of

> *It's not important if things happen for a reason ... they may or may not. We waste countless moments weighing the possibilities. What is important is to find and make reasons for what happens ...*
> —Nic Brooks

it. You may want to try to do one thing from this list each day, or week, or month. You may want to start your own list with family and friends, making a game of trying different things. You may find that you especially enjoy one or two things on this list, and you may just try to do those things as often as possible.

The point is not to try to direct you, persuade you, or recruit you to some kind of "movement." If you want to join a movement, that's great! Find one that works for you or start one yourself. All we are doing is adding to your list of options, showing that you are not as limited as you may have thought.

--- Idea ---

Think about events that you have considered to be unfortunate, and then think about how necessary those events were to put you exactly where you are now.

Chapter Nine

MORE GOOD STUFF

I view these closing words as more of a beginning than an end. Then again, it may be even more accurate to look at them as a continuation of ideas that have existed for centuries. I have attempted to reframe and cross-reference important concepts that may help you to grow and contribute in your own ways. A few readers may even find that our discussions resonate with their personal patterns of thinking. That would be wonderful.

If this book does nothing for you, please pass it on to someone else who may get some use from it. Then, please find your own way to re-energize and re-focus your efforts to "pay it forward." Please consider this: If we treat the negative elements of the world as "someone else's problems," they will soon become everyone's problems. If we treat the negative elements in the world as our own problems, they will eventually become no one's problems!

Thank you for your time and your good thoughts.

A Few Things You Can Do to Change Our World

Please keep in mind that these suggestions are not intended as legal, financial, medical, or spiritual advice. It is up to you and the appropriate professionals to decide what is safe, legal, healthy, and cost-efficient for you. This list is not so much to be read as to be consulted. If you find that you have an extra dollar or an extra hour, it may help you with new ideas about how to invest in world change.

This list is not intended to be read straight through. It is to be used more as a reference guide when you are looking for new ideas.

In one minute or less...

- Learn a new joke and tell it to someone. You know the saying about "the healing power of laughter." That saying appears to have some truth to it.
- Give a sincere compliment to a friend, a relative, a stranger, an employee, a child, a senior citizen, or yourself. Compliments are free, but they do wonders for the spirit.
- Personally thank a soldier, teacher, nurse, artist, musician, crossing guard, police officer, fire fighter, EMT, or any other deserving person.

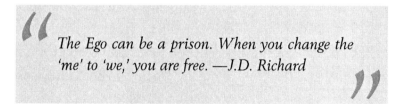

The Ego can be a prison. When you change the 'me' to 'we,' you are free. —J.D. Richard

- Do something to leave every place you visit a little bit better than the way you found it.
- Pick up a piece of trash and throw it away. If everyone did this once per day, litter would no longer be much of a problem.
- Turn off the water when you brush your teeth. This saves more water than you may think.
- Extinguish and properly dispose of your cigarette butts if you smoke. Cigarette butts are litter, just like other trash.
- When you choose to do something, make a decision to do it to the best of your ability. It only takes one moment to make a decision.
- Tell someone special how you feel about them. This is more powerful than you may think.
- Hold the door for someone. Chivalry is not dead—it's just not doing too well these days. We can bring it back from the brink. Showing basic manners can restore hope in humanity for those who observe.
- Smile and greet a stranger.

I find that being productive is the best way to escape my troubles for a while. I always say: 'If you are depressed, go to work!' When I am helping others, I don't have time to think about what is bothering me. —Popy Demertzis

- Ask to leave information about a charity inside a restaurant or store. You never know who may find it and decide to help.
- Drink an extra glass or bottle of water. Hydration is one of the most important keys to health. The healthier you are, the better you can help yourself and others.
- Close your eyes and take a deep breath. Stress kills, and deep breathing reduces stress.
- Bring kindness to a negative situation in any way that you can.
- If possible, bring positive feedback to a negative person.
- If you are of legal age to drink alcohol, set a limit for yourself and stick to it. No one likes a belligerent person.
- Leave your newspaper or magazine where someone else can find and read it (on a bus or train, or in a restaurant).
- Leave an encouraging note for someone in your house or workplace.
- Weigh yourself. Many claim that merely keeping an eye on your weight each day tends to steer you toward sensible eating.
- Let someone in front of you in traffic. This type of kindness helps to lessen "road rage."
- Let a pedestrian cross. Maybe even two.
- Make sure that someone who lets you into traffic or lets you cross the street sees you wave and express thanks. This will encourage him or her to keep up the good work.

- Go out of your way to greet and be kind to people who need information or directions, maintaining a safe distance if it is a stranger.
- Leave a smile behind when you leave a room.
- Write down something you learned today and share it.
- Receive a compliment and enjoy it. Many people deflect compliments because they do not feel worthy of them. Start assuming that all compliments are sincere and well-deserved.
- Be nice to callers who have the wrong number. Everyone makes mistakes.
- Give someone a second chance.
- Give a hug to a friend who needs one. Like smiles and compliments, hugs are free, but they work miracles.
- Remove your food from plastic containers and put it into microwave-safe glass or ceramic before microwaving. According to many experts, microwaving plastic can release dangerous toxins.
- Hold a door for someone.
- Floss your teeth. Reducing chance of infection in your mouth will help you to be healthier and live longer.
- Compliment someone's tattoo or piercings. Many people with body modifications believe that they will be judged. Show that you encourage their self-expression.
- Jot down your own good deeds throughout the day. It is encouraging to see just how many little positive changes you can pack into a day.
- Apologize without expecting forgiveness.

- Forgive without expecting an apology.
- Add to this list. Feel free to use the white space of this book to jot down ideas. Use this as a workbook!

In five minutes or less...

- Stretch your muscles for **five** minutes.
- Breathe deeply and relax your mind for **five** minutes.
- Drop used toys in a "Toys for Tots" bin or other donation drop site.
- Send a friendly e-mail to someone in another country. Remember that we all share the same world. If all nations had citizens who were close friends, many conflicts would be avoided.
- Set up an emergency code word and a safe word for your family. A code word is a word that you all use to communicate that an emergency is in progress and immediate help is needed. A safe word is created so that children know that they can trust someone you have sent for them.
- If you find an umbrella that someone has left behind, carry it with you as a spare to give to someone in the rain who does not have an umbrella.
- Ask a cultural question of someone from another country. This shows that you care about other cultures enough to want to learn about them.
- Always try to be a good guest.
- Don't go to a party empty-handed.
- Listen intently to a story from another culture and think about its meaning.

- When going to another country, ask someone ahead of time if there is anything you can bring to contribute or donate.
- When going to another country, pack items to donate to that country's poor. Every country has underprivileged people.
- When going to another country, write down at least a few key phrases in their language to show that you are polite and respectful of your hosts, their home, and their culture.
- When in another country, go out of your way to be clean and respectful of both public and private spaces.
- Use any binders around the house to fill with used paper. You can make scrap notebooks for notes and doodles rather than wasting paper. Just use the blank sides of the used sheets.
- Post a note on anything public that is broken (vending machines or parking meters, for example) to let operators know that the item needs repair, and to let others know not to waste their money.
- Ask to meet and personally thank a chef or a cook for a great meal. Cooking is often a thankless job, but we all depend on it.
- Set up your printer to do double-sided printing when possible. It is surprising how much paper this saves.

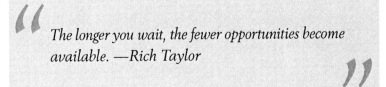

The longer you wait, the fewer opportunities become available. —Rich Taylor

- Buy recycled products when you can, especially when the price is about the same.
- Put an "in case of emergency" number (ICE) in your cell phone. This helps emergency personnel to contact the right people if you are injured. The paramedics and police don't know who the most important people are among the 500 names in your phone.
- When a client sends in a complimenting e-mail about an employee/co-worker, instead of just sharing the e-mail with that person, share it with all of their co-workers as well to spread the positive energy.
- Donate old glasses to a Lion's Club drop box.
- Donate a cell phone to "Cell Phones for Soldiers."
- Collect car keys from friends who have been drinking.
- Call 911 for someone who needs help.
- Call local police to help someone whose vehicle has broken down. It is not always safe to stop to help, but you can make a call to send help.
- Turn off your cell phone in the theatre, cinema, seminars, meetings, and any public performance places.
- Keep your voice down while talking on the cell phone in public places.
- Clean up after your dog.
- Leave a hand-written "thank-you" note for a deserving stranger.
- Set a monthly goal for your good deeds—a "paying it forward" goal.
- Add to this list.

In ten minutes or less...

- Tell a story about how great a friend or co-worker is.
- Take ten minutes to help a local senior citizen.
- Identify a bias or prejudice of your own, and think about where it comes from and if it is rational.
- Offer a blind person your arm when crossing the street. You can politely introduce yourself and ask, "Would you like to take my arm?" Do not be offended if he or she declines. Most people with limited vision are highly trained for mobility in the ways that work best for their condition. Depending on his or her routine, it may actually be easier to walk without your assistance. However, the offer is usually greatly appreciated.
- Take out the recycling.
- When driving, please be courteous to bikers and truckers as well as other passenger cars, vans, and trucks. No matter how late you are, a wreck will make the situation much worse. There is no excuse for driving recklessly or aggressively. It's not a race, unless you are on a track and a green flag has been waved.
- Photocopy everything in your wallet, front and back, and keep it in a safe place in case your wallet is lost or stolen. You will be able to cancel and replace all IDs and credit cards much more easily.
- Post a useful item that you no longer need on the Internet for free. "Free-cycling" groups are great for this.
- Ask someone to share a story of personal success, and really listen.

- Share a story of personal success with someone who wants to hear it.
- Talk to kids about bullying. Spend more time listening than talking.
- Talk to kids about drugs. Spend more time listening than talking.
- Talk to kids about their video games. Spend more time listening than talking.
- Take time to help an international visitor find a place or service.
- Ask questions about another culture, and listen.
- Let a child teach you something.
- Let a senior citizen teach you something.
- Let a friend teach you something.
- Call a local college and ask for recommendations of responsible students to help with household chores and business tasks.
- Take out trash in the morning, if possible. This makes it harder for criminals to steal your trash and go through it for information.
- Pick up the garbage on your street for ten minutes.
- Allow friends to "sign out" useful items you have. Even people with the best of intentions forget to return things, but having a "sign-out" system helps you to keep track of who has what.
- Donate magazines to a school art program.
- Write to compliment a company that is ethical and professional.

- Write to compliment a celebrity who is ethical and professional.
- Write to compliment a leader who is ethical and professional.
- Get up early and go outside just to listen to the birds sing.
- Sign up to be an organ donor, if it is in alignment with your religious beliefs.
- Post positive responses to blogs.
- Add to this list.

In one hour or less...

- Donate clothing and other items to a local charity.
- Donate a dead vehicle to a charity (and enjoy the tax write off).
- Check the curb on trash night to see if anyone is throwing out anything that can be used, repaired, or donated. People tend to be VERY wasteful. I have found perfect lamps that just needed new bulbs!
- Make a list of changes that you would like to see in the world.
- Make a list of things that you can do to help bring about the changes you want to see in the world.
- Do one of the things from your list of changes that you want to see in the world.
- Volunteer to walk or interact with dogs at a shelter.
- Volunteer to interact with cats at a shelter.
- Write a poem and read it to someone.

- Bake or cook for someone who will be helped by your effort.
- Shop at an online store linked to a charity. This is a great way to give back without costing you extra money.
- Donate blood.
- Set up a visit to a nursing home.
- Visit kids or seniors in the hospital.
- Donate hair from your haircut to Locks of Love or a similar organization.
- Attend a multicultural event.
- Attend an event where you are the minority. This is a great way to chip away at racial and cultural barriers.
- Attend a school play. Plays are hard work, and everyone involved will appreciate your support.
- Always attend a funeral if humanly possible. It is important for the family to know that you care.
- Attend a music recital where you know no one. Enjoy the music for what it is, not merely to placate those who talked you into showing up.
- Attend a school athletic event where you know no one.
- Visit a place of worship for a religion other than your own.
- Read an article or watch a documentary about another religion.
- Read an article or watch a documentary about another culture.
- Read about alkalizing. Many experts claim that an alkaline body chemistry is an important key to health. Consult

your physician, do your own research, and decide for yourself.

- Attend an educational seminar about anything.
- Attend an art exhibit and talk to the artist(s). You can always learn something from art, even if it is not "your style."
- Shovel a neighbor's driveway and/or sidewalk, taking all necessary safety precautions.
- Watch or read news from another country.
- If you are of legal age to drink alcohol, arrange for a designated driver when you go out.
- Be a designated driver.
- Arrange to be an emergency driver if a friend finds he or she cannot drive home.
- Try anything new that is safe and legal.
- Read to a group of kids.
- Talk with a Scout troop about an area of your expertise.
- Learn to make something useful from materials you would normally discard.
- Donate old carpeting for use in a dorm, doghouse, play set, or any other use.
- Play a game with a senior, a kid, a friend.
- Donate old movies, music, and books to those who want and appreciate them.

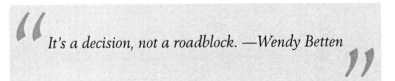

It's a decision, not a roadblock. —Wendy Betten

- Visit a library and look at books related to subjects you know nothing about. Expand out of your intellectual comfort zone.
- Ask someone you trust for advice about something important to you.
- Repair and use something you were about to throw away.
- Listen to an opposing view on politics or religion without arguing or judging.
- Mow the lawn of a senior or a person with health problems.
- Play the "six degrees of separation" game.
- List ten major goals for your life.
- List ten things you can do to move toward achieving each of your goals.
- Help a friend list ten things that that person can do to achieve his or her goals.
- Shop at local stores when you need to buy a gift.
- Recycle your dead batteries, or use rechargeable ones.
- Learn a new route to work or school. Options are always good, and an alternate route can save time and stress.
- Learn a public transportation route to work or school. If the car is out of commission, it is great to have another way to do what you need to do. Furthermore, using public transportation may be more ecologically sound.
- Participate in a neighborhood watch program.
- Add to this list.

In two hours or less...

- Have a "swap meet" party. This kind of party involves everyone bringing useful or nice items that they no longer use and giving them away freely.

- Volunteer to speak at a school about your job or hobby. You have more knowledge than you think, so spread it around!

- Read or listen to part of a book on success, personal growth, or spirituality.

- Show the funniest movie you have ever seen to a group of friends.

- Show the most inspirational movie you have ever seen to a group of friends.

- Learn to make something new with your hands. This can be both practical and therapeutic.

- Attend a gathering where you know few people and really try to find commonalities.

- Watch *Pay it Forward*.

- Watch *Second-Hand Lions*.

- Watch *The Secret*.

With writing, there seems to be a lot of rules in terms of 'what's allowed.' I think these rules can be all broken into shards, if you do it well enough.
—Jason Falcione

- Guys: Watch a "chick flick" with your wife or girlfriend, if she likes those films.
- Ladies: Watch an action film with your husband or boyfriend if he enjoys those movies.
- Watch *What the Bleep Do We Know?*
- Watch *August Rush.*
- Watch *Simon Birch.*
- Watch *The Straight Story.*
- Watch a film with your kid(s) and then talk about how it applies to his or her life.
- Throw a "good news" party—a gathering that focuses on positive events and positive energy, no complaining allowed. You can toast to positive things going on in your lives or in the world, announce lucky finds, promotions, weddings, births, and so on.
- Watch a movie that you know will make you cry.
- Have a salvaging party. Get together with friends to fix or improve broken, ripped, or otherwise messed-up items.
- List ten reasons to be proud of your job and write a paragraph about why each reason is important and helpful in the world.
- List ten reasons to be proud of your life and write a paragraph about why each of these things is important to you and to others. Continue to add to the list.
- List ten reasons to be proud of your family and write a paragraph about each person who has made you proud. Then, share this writing with those on the list.

- Spend two hours teaching all you can to a person trying to learn your language.
- Be a designated driver for an event.
- Try to find a pen pal / Internet pal in another country. Establish friendly correspondence, focusing on goodwill and commonalities.
- Learn polite greetings in as many languages as possible.
- Add to this list.

In one day or less…
- Volunteer for The Brother's Brother Foundation or a similar charity where you package surplus medical supplies to save lives in distressed countries. (I love this idea!)
- Volunteer at a soup kitchen.
- Volunteer at an animal shelter.
- Volunteer at the Habitat for Humanity.
- Volunteer anywhere!
- Have a crafting party to make useful items from things you would normally discard, such as boxes, newspapers, milk cartons, milk jugs, bottles, and cans.

Man, if you can't get out of bed in the morning thankful for another day and feeling at least a little excited about the challenges the day may bring, then do everyone a favor and stay in bed. Negativity is contagious, like the flu. —Andy Kapolka

- Research and attend the best self-defense and crime prevention classes you can find.
- Buy in bulk when possible to save money and cut down on wasteful packaging.
- Take a nature-based class outdoors to study forestry, bird watching, or ecology.
- Help a friend move, asking in return only that he or she "pays it forward."
- Have a group garage sale and donate the profits.
- After achieving a major goal, take one day to relax and regroup.
- Learn CPR, First Aid, blood-born pathogen handling, and defibrillator usage.
- Offer your skills for free for one day to a person who is disabled, elderly, or otherwise limited.
- If you have kids, spend the day with them interacting with animals in some way. Animals are a litmus test of the personality. The way people treat animals usually tells you a good deal about their personalities and the way they treat people (including themselves). Encouraging kids to be kind to animals is a great way to develop the traits of kindness, compassion, and responsibility.
- Read a Utopian novel.
- You guessed it! Add to this list!

For $1 or less…
- Tape a $1 bill where someone will find it with a note that says something like: "Dear friend, Please take this money and use it in a way that will make your life easier today."

I guarantee you that person's life will change just a tiny bit from this senseless act of minor generosity.

- Buy a small pocket notebook and record every kind action you observe.
- Pay $1 to a kid you know for telling you a story or singing a song. This encourages the child to be expressive, and it can be pretty entertaining!
- Carry a $1 food item to give to a homeless person. You can't really go wrong with giving food to a hungry person.
- Send a "Thank You" card to someone for something small.
- Buy from a bake sale, lemonade stand, or other local fundraiser or kid's business.
- Tip a street musician. They deserve it.
- Pay someone's toll. They may be confused, but they will certainly be impressed by your kindness. Hopefully, they will do the same thing for someone else some day.
- Put money in someone's parking meter.
- Put a buck in a collection jar, box, or can.
- Always donate at least $1 to fire fighters or police fundraisers, if you can.

> *I try to keep an open mind towards everyone. Some of the nicest people I have met have been people I first thought different.* —*John Poremski*

- Donate at least $1 to environmental projects.
- Throw a buck in the tip jar for any service.
- Give an extra $1 tip for a server.

For $5 or less...

- Pay someone's bus or train fare. You can just give the driver extra money and ask him or her to apply it to the next riders.
- Give a cab driver an extra $5 to put toward the next person's fare with a simple message like: "Have a great day."
- Send a random person a $5 gift card anonymously.
- Buy and use reusable grocery bags.
- Buy an inexpensive but thoughtful present for someone for no reason.
- Buy a few extra cards for occasions that you know will come up eventually.
- Buy a few extra "occasion cards" for friends who tend to forget to send cards.
- Make a "dummy wallet." Buy a cheap wallet and fill it with junk that cannot be traced back to you—blank cards that they send to you with credit card offers and receipts without credit card info. If, God forbid, someone robs you, throw him the dummy wallet and run. By the time he figures out that it's worthless, you will have made it to safety.
- Tip a street musician *well*. What a wonderful world it would be if every corner had happy, talented people playing their hearts out for an appreciative crowd!

- Buy a durable plastic or metal mug with a lid to carry with you all the time (just throw it in your bag or your car) for coffee, tea, or water. This helps to reduce the waste of disposable cups.
- Anonymously pay for a stranger's coffee, donut, or drive-through order with the message "pay it forward."
- Buy a used or discounted book as a gift for someone who will be helped by it.

For $10 or less...

- Leave $10 for your postal worker when it is not a holiday. These guys work pretty hard.
- Donate to any charity. It really adds up.
- Buy an inexpensive corded phone for your house if you have only cordless phones. The corded phone is useful when the power goes out but the phone lines are up.
- Pay a breakfast or lunch check for a lone diner, especially a person in uniform. Ask the server or cashier not to tell

I literally have to make a point to call myself out from time to time. It's the only way I'm able to stay on top of it. I try to be as honest with myself as I can to really understand why I have the feelings I do and apply them in a positive way. I have to realize that it's not someone else's fault if I feel insecure or unworthy because of the way someone else presents themselves or acts. —Mike Cortese

who you are, but to say that a stranger just wanted that person to have a good day. If it is a stranger in uniform, you may want to pass on the message: "Thank you for your service to our country (community/world)."

- Hang bells on the door handles at the entrances of your home—different sounding bells for different doors. You will soon be able to tell not only if someone is coming or going, but which door is being used. This is good for security and for keeping track of kids and even pets.
- Send an anonymous care package to a friend who is having a tough week.
- Give a $10 gift card to a shelter.
- Buy a $10 phone card to give to a shelter or person in need.
- Print out a list of free, helpful, and life-saving services to leave in local businesses. For example, poison control, suicide hotline, single mother hotline, security escorts, or free counselors.
- Give a care package to a shelter with personal items like new socks and underwear, razors, a mirror, a brush, a comb, a toothbrush, deodorant, and a kind note of encouragement.

For $100 or less...

Now we are getting into a level of money where some people start to feel a bit less generous. Depending on your income level and your comfort level, $100 may seem like a fortune, or it may seem like nothing. If it seems like a fortune, please don't dismiss this category too hastily. No one said how long it may take to accumulate this money or that it all had to come from you. You could save pocket change for a year to come up with $100, or you could have ten friends chip in $10 apiece. How about twenty friends or relatives chipping in $5? This gets back to one of the core ideas of this project: a bunch of "little bits" add up to a whole lot. You don't have to be the whole solution. No one is! Just be a small, but vital, part of the solution.

- Donate to a local charity.
- Donate to any charity.
- Give $100 anonymously to a person you know who really needs the financial help.
- Buy a rebounder (mini trampoline) for your home and jog or jump on it while watching TV or playing video games. Most people dislike aerobic exercise because it's boring. On a rebounder, you can jog, bounce, or walk while doing other things. (Consult your physician before doing any kind of exercise, of course.)

> *Although I have yet to turn my dreams into reality, your dream is your dream. It's what drives people. You can't let people talk you out of that because it's not their dream. Therefore, they cannot fully understand it nor appreciate it. Maybe it's not their fault when they criticize. It's that they are not looking through your eyes. —Angel*

- Send toys or other items to a charity overseas. There are so many people who desperately need things that are lying around your house. Contact the charities online and see what they need, and then collect items and ship them out with a note, pictures, or anything you like. This is a great group activity, and the shipping charge will be the only expense. For $100, you can ship a good-sized package overseas to many places.
- Buy a headset for your home phone so that you can free your hands to clean, wash dishes, and exercise while catching up with friends. This allows you to be much more efficient, freeing up time for other things.
- Put together a care package for a soldier.
- Get a water filtration system for your home.
- Buy the best language program you can find to expand your knowledge of another tongue … and use it!

If you do not feel great after doing a bunch of these things, even the small ones, keep at it! Sometimes it takes a while to find what really "clicks" for you.

Force will never triumph over logic. —Josh Tamburo

More Words of Wisdom

"It's my entrepreneurial spirit which drives me. I can't explain it any other way, but once I set my mind to something, I have to see it through to the end. There's always a reward or satisfaction at the end or along the way that fuels my fire." —Dean Hastings

"There are over six billion people in this world. If you have any idea, good or bad, chances are awesome that you can find someone that is crazy enough to think that it is a bad idea. The world is full of 'armchair consultants' who have never attempted to accomplish your dream, but will be quick to tell you why your dream is impossible. My rule of thumb is, 'If you haven't tried it, you can't advise on it.'" —Bob Dickey

"The biggest drive that I get is when I am at my lowest point and I come to realize that I still have life, people who love me, and a place to live, and also that every morning I wake up on this side of the grass." —Matt Fastuca

"If it feels good, think first, then do it." —Larry "The Captain," Schifko

"I try to understand that everybody is their own unique person and probably has a good reason for what they do, even if I don't understand it. For example, if somebody cuts me off on the road, that person may be in a hurry to get to the hospital to see their sick mom." —Bill J. Laboon

"My policy is to simply 'Keep it real.'" —Phil Laboon

"If you open your heart, the world for you will change and never be as it was before." —Paul Dodge

"I want to make a difference in my world and lead by example for my kids, and as a legacy. I want to know that I have made a difference in some way." —Cooper Munroe

"I think the way I do due to some innate sense of guidance, brought upon by an unknown source." —Joe Thomas

"Don't let fear control your life—thank God for the abilities and talent you have been given that you take for granted every day." —S.P.

"When I help someone, I don't expect anything in return. When someone helps me, I appreciate it." —Bill W. Laboon, "Boom Boom"

"Approaching a stranger with a smile or just being nice to someone usually sets a positive mood. Prejudice is based on your own background. As you age, you get to meet people outside your circle and realize that the majority of people are really good at heart." —Kathy Laboon

"Never lend money with the expectation of receiving it back, and you will never be disappointed." —Paul Cannon

"Don't dwell on the negative. Dwell on getting past it." —Sami Howes

"In my world, there is no place or time for racial and religious intolerance. EVERYONE is measured against the same yardstick, and that is how you are you squared away. In my world, nobody cares what color you are, just what blood type you have." –P.A. McAleer; *Dedicated to Larry "Wild Weasel" Young —KIA 22 MAY 09, Baghdad, Iraq*

"I'm a stubborn guy. I refuse to give up if I believe something is worthwhile. At the same time, I will always size something up and decide whether there is a real opportunity." —Jose Dino

"To be driven enough to want to turn a dream into reality means that that person sees that the status quo is not good enough, and it is like a unsettled inner 'nagging' that will be lingering with them until they at least make a genuine effort to make their dream a reality ..." —Mike Accomando

"It's not that hard to be nice to others, even if it takes a ten-second breather to get over frustration. I think that a lot of people don't go out of their way to be nice because of their habits of going their own way, doing their own thing, and not wanting to stick out ... But if we could live in the immortality of our beings, maybe we'd realize that it's the small kindnesses that really matter." —Emily Danchuck

"It's the random moments in your life that are always the most significant." —Holly Yoder

"People ask me all the time, 'Why are you always smiling?' I tell them because I love life. I truly do love life! I try to find the

positive aspect in even the craziest situations. I try to surround myself with people that are positive ... I love all my friends and I want to see them succeed and make good decisions in life. If you could somehow place a monetary value on friends, I would be a trillionaire!" —Ed Schoeb

"Please let the people I love outlive me, because they are the only things I can't live without." —Bob Ward

"You can change the world by doing something that seems so very miniscule to you, but means the world to someone else." —Keith Click

"Whenever I'm feeling stressed or anti-human, I try to think of something I am grateful for in the situation. For example, if I am having a bad day at work, I think about the people who don't even have jobs." —Anonymous

"If you want to get something done, you will make it happen; if you don't, you will find an excuse. We rationalize our short-comings way too much as humans and let ourselves be mediocre simply because that is the easy thing to do." —Charley Johnson

"To those who fight for it, life has a flavor the protected never know." —Motto of the Board of the Atlanta Vietnam Veterans Business Association, provided by Mark Steele

TO LEARN MORE

hese are merely suggestions, and some of the readings listed here may not fit with your beliefs or personal interests. The point of listing these works, and the point of this entire book, is to suggest many of the options you may not have been aware of. The biggest challenge in creating this list was to keep it pretty short. We could fill an entire book with suggested readings!

We have come to believe that the books listed can be very informative and enlightening, especially if they do not fit perfectly with your present worldview. For instance, the spiritually-oriented books listed are not here to convert you or to change your beliefs, but merely to help you to see how others have come to form their own beliefs. This may help you to become more sympathetic, understanding, and a better communicator with those who think differently. These books are on a wide variety of subjects, and we are not claiming that these are the best sources in the world. The idea is to shoot more options your way so that you can make up your own mind about what is good for you. There may be various editions, so we have presented only authors and titles.

A Few Suggested Readings:

Baroody, Theodore A. *Alkalize or Die*

Bookspan, Jolie. Fix *Your Own Pain Without Drugs or Surgery*

Byrne, Rhonda. *The Secret*

Canfield, Jack. *Chicken Soup for the Soul*

Clason, George S. *The Richest Man in Babylon*

Covey, Stephen R. *The 8th Habit*

Douglas, Frederick. *Narrative of the Life of Frederick Douglass, an American Slave*

Fox, Michael J. *Always Looking Up: The Adventures of an Incurable Optimist*

Hawking, Stephen. *A Brief History of Time*

Hesse, Herman. *Siddhartha*

Hicks, Esther and Jerry. *The Law of Attraction*

Hill, Napoleon. *Think & Grow Rich*

Huxley, Aldous. *The Perennial Philosophy*

Hyde, Catherine Ryan. *Pay it Forward*

Lenehan, Arthur F. (editor) *The Best of Bits and Pieces*

Loewen, James W. *Lies My Teacher Told Me*

Moore, Sir Thomas. *Utopia*

Nightingale, Earl. *The Strangest Secret for Succeeding in the World Today*

Qubein, Nido. *How to Get Anything You Want*

Robbins, Anthony. *Get the Edge*

Rossi, M.L. *What Every American Should Know About the Rest of the World*

Schultz, Patricia. *1,000 Places to See Before You Die*

Stock, Gregory. *The Book of Questions*

vos Savante, Marilyn and Leonore Fleischer. *Brain Building*

Thoreau, Henry David. *Walden*

Walker, Alice. *The Color Purple*

Walsh, Neal Donald. *Conversations with God, Happier than God*

Warren, Rick. *The Purpose Driven Life*

Ziglar, Zig. *See You at the Top*

www.DoingGoodWorks.org